B Osceola

Bland, Celia.

Osceola : Seminole rebel

OSCEOLA

―――――――――――▼ ▼ ▼―――――――――――

NORTH AMERICAN INDIANS OF ACHIEVEMENT

OSCEOLA
Seminole Rebel

▼ ▼ ▼

Celia Bland

Senior Consulting Editor
W. David Baird
Howard A. White Professor of History
Pepperdine University

CHELSEA HOUSE PUBLISHERS

New York   Philadelphia

FRONTISPIECE A 19th-century engraving depicts Osceola pausing in the course of battle.

ON THE COVER *Osceola, The Black Drink, A Warrior of Great Distinction* (1838) by George Catlin.

Chelsea House Publishers
EDITORIAL DIRECTOR Richard Rennert
EXECUTIVE MANAGING EDITOR Karyn Gullen Browne
EXECUTIVE EDITOR Sean Dolan
COPY CHIEF Robin James
PICTURE EDITOR Adrian G. Allen
ART DIRECTOR Robert Mitchell
MANUFACTURING DIRECTOR Gerald Levine
SYSTEMS MANAGER Lindsey Ottman
PRODUCTION COORDINATOR Marie Claire Cebrián-Ume

North American Indians of Achievement
SENIOR EDITOR Marian W. Taylor

Staff for OSCEOLA
ASSISTANT EDITOR Margaret Dornfeld
EDITORIAL ASSISTANT Joy Sanchez
SENIOR DESIGNER Rae Grant
PICTURE RESEARCHER Lisa Kirchner

Printed and bound in Mexico.

First Printing

1 3 5 7 9 8 6 4 2

Library of Congress Cataloging-in-Publication Data

Bland, Celia.
Osceola: Seminole rebel / Celia Bland; senior consulting editor, W. David Baird.
  p. cm. — (North American Indians of Achievement)
Summary: Describes the life and times of the Seminole chief and warrior who struggled to prevent the removal of his people from their land in Florida.
ISBN 0-7910-1716-8
ISBN 0-7910-1993-4 (pbk.)
1. Osceola, Seminole chief, 1804–1838—Juvenile literature. 2. Seminole Indians—Biography—Juvenile literature. 3. Seminole Indians—History—Juvenile literature. [1. Osceola, Seminole chief, 1804–1838. 2. Seminole Indians—Biography. 3. Indians of North America—Florida—Biography.] I. Baird, W. David. II. Title. III. Series.
E99.S280814 1993   93-21750
973'.04973'0092—dc20   CIP
  [B]   AC

CONTENTS

NORTH AMERICAN INDIANS OF ACHIEVEMENT

BLACK HAWK
Sac Rebel

JOSEPH BRANT
Mohawk Chief

COCHISE
Apache Chief

CRAZY HORSE
Sioux War Chief

CHIEF GALL
Sioux War Chief

GERONIMO
Apache Warrior

HIAWATHA
Founder of the Iroquois
Confederacy

CHIEF JOSEPH
Nez Perce Leader

PETER MACDONALD
Former Chairman of the Navajo
Nation

WILMA MANKILLER
Principal Chief of the Cherokees

OSCEOLA
Seminole Rebel

QUANAH PARKER
Comanche Chief

KING PHILIP
Wampanoag Rebel

POCAHONTAS
Powhatan Peacemaker

PONTIAC
Ottawa Rebel

RED CLOUD
Sioux War Chief

WILL ROGERS
Cherokee Entertainer

SITTING BULL
Chief of the Sioux

TECUMSEH
Shawnee Rebel

JIM THORPE
Sac and Fox Athlete

SARAH WINNEMUCCA
Northern Paiute Writer and
Diplomat

Other titles in preparation

ON INDIAN LEADERSHIP

by W. David Baird

Howard A. White Professor of History
Pepperdine University

Authoritative utterance is in thy mouth, perception is in thy heart, and thy tongue is the shrine of justice," the ancient Egyptians said of their king. From him, the Egyptians expected authority, discretion, and just behavior. Homer's *Iliad* suggests that the Greeks demanded somewhat different qualities from their leaders: justice and judgment, wisdom and counsel, shrewdness and cunning, valor and action. It is not surprising that different people living at different times should seek different qualities from the individuals they looked to for guidance. By and large, a people's requirements for leadership are determined by two factors: their culture and the unique circumstances of the time and place in which they live.

Before the late 15th century, when non-Indians first journeyed to what is now North America, most Indian tribes were not ruled by a single person. Instead, there were village chiefs, clan headmen, peace chiefs, war chiefs, and a host of other types of leaders, each with his or her own specific duties. These influential people not only decided political matters but also helped shape their tribe's social, cultural, and religious life. Usually, Indian leaders held their positions because they had won the respect of their peers. Indeed, if a leader's followers at any time decided that he or she was out of step with the will of the people, they felt free to look to someone else for advice and direction.

Thus, the greatest achievers in traditional Indian communities were men and women of extraordinary talent. They were not only skilled at navigating the deadly waters of tribal politics and cultural customs but also able to, directly or indirectly, make a positive and significant difference in the daily life of their followers.

From the beginning of their interaction with Native Americans, non-Indians failed to understand these features of Indian leadership. Early European explorers and settlers merely assumed that Indians had the same relationship with their leaders as non-Indians had with their kings and queens. European monarchs generally inherited their positions and ruled large nations however they chose, often with little regard for the desires or needs of their subjects. As a result, the settlers of Jamestown saw Pocahontas as a "princess" and Pilgrims dubbed Wampanoag leader Metacom "King Philip," envisioning them in roles very different from those in which their own people placed them.

As more and more non-Indians flocked to North America, the nature of Indian leadership gradually began to change. Influential Indians no longer had to take on the often considerable burden of pleasing only their own people; they also had to develop a strategy of dealing with the non-Indian newcomers. In a rapidly changing world, new types of Indian role models with new ideas and talents continually emerged. Some were warriors; others were peacemakers. Some held political positions within their tribes; others were writers, artists, religious prophets, or athletes. Although the demands of Indian leadership altered from generation to generation, several factors that determined which Indian people became prominent in the centuries after first contact remained the same.

Certain personal characteristics distinguished these Indians of achievement. They were intelligent, imaginative, practical, daring, shrewd, uncompromising, ruthless, and logical. They were constant in friendships, unrelenting in hatreds, affectionate with their relatives, and respectful to their God or gods. Of course, no single Native American leader embodied all these qualities, nor these qualities only. But it was these characteristics that allowed them to succeed.

The special skills and talents that certain Indians possessed also brought them to positions of importance. The life of Hiawatha, the legendary founder of the powerful Iroquois Confederacy, displays the value that oratorical ability had for many Indians in power.

The biography of Cochise, the 19th-century Apache chief, illustrates that leadership often required keen diplomatic skills not only in transactions among tribespeople but also in hardheaded negotiations with non-Indians. For others, such as Mohawk Joseph Brant and Navajo Peter MacDonald, a non-Indian education proved advantageous in their dealings with other peoples.

Sudden changes in circumstance were another crucial factor in determining who became influential in Indian communities. King Philip in the 1670s and Geronimo in the 1880s both came to power when their people were searching for someone to lead them into battle against white frontiersmen who had forced upon them a long series of indignities. Seeing the rising discontent of Indians of many tribes in the 1810s, Tecumseh and his brother, the Shawnee prophet Tenskwatawa, proclaimed a message of cultural revitalization that appealed to thousands. Other Indian achievers recognized cooperation with non-Indians as the most advantageous path during their lifetime. Sarah Winnemucca in the late 19th century bridged the gap of understanding between her people and their non-Indian neighbors through the publication of her autobiography *Life Among the Piutes*. Olympian Jim Thorpe in the early 20th century championed the assimilationist policies of the U.S. government and, with his own successes, demonstrated the accomplishments Indians could make in the non-Indian world. And Wilma Mankiller, principal chief of the Cherokees, continues to fight successfully for the rights of her people through the courts and through negotiation with federal officials.

Leadership among Native Americans, just as among all other peoples, can be understood only in the context of culture and history. But the centuries that Indians have had to cope with invasions of foreigners in their homelands have brought unique hardships and obstacles to the Native American individuals who most influenced and inspired others. Despite these challenges, there has never been a lack of Indian men and women equal to these tasks. With such strong leaders, it is no wonder that Native Americans remain such a vital part of this nation's cultural landscape.

1

"This Is My Mark"

The Florida air was thick with tension. Under a makeshift pavilion at Fort King, a small government outpost in the northern interior of the territory, 22 leaders from the Seminole Indian nation had gathered to discuss the fate of their people. Standing opposite them were General Duncan L. Clinch, commander of Florida troops, and Wiley Thompson, a former general and the agent of the Seminole reservation.

Thompson had worked with the Seminoles for the past year and a half, monitoring their activities and distributing at regular intervals the goods and currency the United States had offered them in partial compensation for land they had recently ceded to the country's white settlers. Once ranging over the entire Florida peninsula, the Seminoles had given up most of their original land in exchange for 4 million acres of marshy soil in the center of the region, a supply of equipment and livestock, an annual payment, and a promise that they would be left in peace. On this April day in 1835, Thompson's task was to make them give up Florida altogether.

The Seminole chiefs were weary and embittered. More than a decade of land disputes, dubious treaties, and

Seminole patriot Osceola is shown in a Florida landscape in this painting by W. M. Laning. Osceola's courage and conviction left a deep impression even on those who opposed him.

11

bloodshed lay behind them. Although the reservation was meant to protect them, most Seminoles who had moved there lived in fear of attack by settlers, the military, and bounty hunters convinced that the tribe was harboring runaway slaves. Disoriented by the threat of removal and burdened with a tract of land where game was scarce and the soil unworkable, many of the Indians had barely survived the recent winter. The chiefs had little from which to draw the strength they needed for resistance.

Their main hope lay in unity, and this, for a people accustomed to long negotiations accommodating each of the tribe's leaders, was hard to come by. Many of the chiefs present at the April meeting had a history of friendship with U.S. officials and of compliance with government demands. Though they had seen the United States fail to honor its agreements, they had so far been hesitant to break their ties and oppose its authority. Friendship aside, the U.S. Army was a powerful force, and the Indians feared it. It was only in recent years, with the government's demand that the Seminoles leave their homeland, that a strong voice of resistance had begun to emerge.

U.S. officials, meanwhile, preferred to recognize the more cooperative chiefs as spokesmen for the tribe. The most prominent of these was Micanopy, a slow-witted, 300-pound man who was not known, even among his own people, as a gifted leader. Jumper, or Otee Emathla, characterized by one officer as "crafty and designing," had acted as Micanopy's mediator in many of his dealings with the whites. Neither of these chiefs agreed wholeheartedly with the U.S. government's Indian policies, but they had so far been unable to take a firm stand against a power they greatly feared.

In 1823, Micanopy and Jumper had been present at Moultrie Creek, near the eastern city of St. Augustine,

Micanopy, a sluggish man of divided sympathies, was about 50 years old when General Wiley Thompson summoned him to Fort King. The U.S. government had come to regard Micanopy as head chief of the Seminoles.

when the document requiring the tribe to leave their villages and resettle in the sandy, wet land of central Florida was signed. Seven years later, at Payne's Landing on the Oklawaha River, the same chiefs had—according to government officials—placed their marks on a treaty requiring the Seminoles to give up that land. Micanopy and his interpreter had traveled west with a small Seminole delegation to evaluate the new territory that the government was promising in exchange for the old. Hundreds of miles from their Florida home and surrounded by the property of their enemies the Creeks, this new land had appeared to them cold and uninviting. Yet meeting with a group of Indian commissioners at nearby Fort Gibson, they had given in to threats from the white negotiators and signed a paper approving the offer.

While U.S. leaders negotiated for their removal, most Seminoles continued to live quietly in small villages along the rivers and streams of the Florida peninsula.

Armed with this battery of written agreements, Wiley Thompson now stood before the Seminole assembly and urged the Indians to enter into yet another agreement. Thompson knew trouble was lurking somewhere in the Seminoles' midst. No sooner had the Fort Gibson representatives returned to their Florida villages than they had begun to declare the treaties they had signed invalid. Micanopy now claimed that his Payne's Landing signature was forged and that the treaty had in any case only been obtained from the Indians through deception. At Fort Gibson, he and other Seminole leaders maintained, they had only intended to show their approval of the land in Indian Territory, not their intention to move there. Besides, they said, their delegation had possessed no authority to sign agreements affecting the Seminole nation as a whole.

Advised of this new tone of defiance, Thompson had hoped to draw from the Indians a pledge of cooperation. In October 1834 he had summoned the Seminoles to a preliminary council at Fort King, which stood near his headquarters at the northern end of the reservation. There, acting on orders from President Andrew Jackson, he had issued an ultimatum: If the Indians did not leave Florida by the following spring, the army would remove them by force.

Much to Thompson's discomfort, the threat did not succeed. Worse yet, the tactic seemed to have unearthed among the chiefs a new and rather unnerving opponent. Upon hearing Thompson's speech, the Indians had asked if they could meet together in private. The agent had assented, then sent an informer to listen in on the meeting. When the spy returned, he told Thompson that a young warrior, a relative newcomer to the Seminole leadership, had dominated the scene, spoken vehemently against the removal plan, and exhorted his compatriots to defy the agent's authority. Thompson's alarm only increased when, after two days of deliberations, the council reconvened. Unanimously, the Seminoles announced that the laws guaranteeing them their Florida land still held, that all later treaties had been fraudulent, and that they had no intention of honoring the president's order to remove. Even Micanopy, who had proved so accommodating in the past, seemed determined to resist expulsion.

Thompson had fumed. The president would compel them to go, he told them, "in irons, if necessary." Furthermore, he said, they would receive no more of their promised annuities until they did. In the brief pause that followed, a warrior had risen to speak for the Seminoles. He was a slender man of dignified bearing, refined features, and spectacular dress. Thompson had noticed the man whispering advice to Micanopy, but until that moment he had never heard him speak. The warrior's voice, when he did, was shrill and passionate. "My brothers!" the Seminole cried in his native Muskogee. "The white man says I shall go, and he will send people to make me go; but I have a rifle, and I have some powder and some lead. I say, we must not leave our homes and lands. If any of our people want to go west we won't let them; and I tell them they are our enemies, and we will treat them so, for the Great Spirit will protect us."

Thompson had met his adversary. This firebrand, known to the whites as Osceola, had been rising in the ranks of Seminole leaders for the past several years. Thompson apprehended him in anger and in fear. Seeking to forestall a crisis, he had granted the Seminoles still more time to consider their response to Jackson's order. Meanwhile, in his report to the commissioner of Indian affairs, he had written of his encounter with Osceola, expressing his uneasiness over this "bold and dashing young chief . . . vehemently opposed to removal."

Jackson, who was handed this report, responded by summarily scrawling across its back: "Let a sufficient military force be forthwith ordered to protect our citizens." Jackson had never been against using violence to attain his ends. The United States was preparing itself for war.

When the council resumed, then, on April 23, 1835, much was at stake for Seminoles and whites alike. Thompson and his authoritative companion Clinch may have hoped that time had weakened the tribe's resolve. Indeed, falling in line with the government's strategy, the Seminole leaders' push for resistance had lost some of its momentum.

A number of futile talks had taken place in the interim. The day before, the Seminoles had heard the removal message in the president's own words, for Jackson had written an address to the Indians for Thompson to read aloud. On hearing the speech, which told the Seminoles nothing new, Jumper had stood up to reaffirm the tribe's opposition to the plan. Jumper was well known for his abilities as a speaker, but Thompson did not like what he heard. Thompson had lashed out at Jumper and those who had supported his speech. Clinch, for his part, had assured the group that he had the power to make them comply and had every intention of using it. The discussion had dissolved for the day.

Now Thompson stood before the Seminole leaders once again, gesturing to the table beside him, on which a document was spread. The paper confirmed the Indians' agreement to give up Florida peacefully, as specified in the earlier Treaty of Payne's Landing. Thompson asked the chiefs to sign.

Intimidated by the thought of an army attack, several

chiefs reluctantly lined up to place their marks on the treaty. Then, slowly, a confused murmur of dissent rose from the Seminoles. At length, four of the chiefs, Jumper among them, announced that the agent had threatened them in vain: they would never give up their Florida homeland; they would not sign the treaty. Micanopy, as Thompson soon learned, had refused even to attend the meeting. The officials had received word that the "head chief" no longer recognized the decisions made at Payne's Landing, and that he would not stir from land that was his by rights. Enraged, Thompson abruptly struck the names of the five insubordinates from his roster of chiefs and announced that the United States would no longer regard them as leaders of the Seminole Nation.

What followed has acquired the status of legend. Infuriated with the agent's actions, the Indians burst out in a roar of protest. One chief whose name had been scratched from the list stamped his feet and gnashed his

Osceola drives his knife into Wiley Thompson's treaty, a document that would oblige the Seminoles to abandon Florida.

teeth in anger. Clinch's attendants braced themselves for a skirmish. Finally, according to a popular account, the one Seminole whose strength and tenacity Thompson had been loath to contend with announced his presence. Osceola, in the cool, determined manner for which he would come to be known, strode toward the table at Thompson's side, drew out his knife, and plunged it through the document, pinning it to the bargaining table. "This is my mark!" he cried. "I will make no other."

2

Runaways

Osceola had not always been a Seminole, nor had he always lived in Florida. He was born in the Upper Creek town of Tallassee, near present-day Tuskegee, Alabama, around 1804. Like many Creek Indians of his generation, he came of mixed parentage, though he would later proudly deny his white heritage. His great-grandfather, Scottish hunter James McQueen, had settled with the Tallassee Indians in the Tallapoosa River valley in 1716. An intelligent and handsome man who greatly respected the Native American way of life, McQueen married a Tallassee woman, adopted tribal customs, and became a respected interpreter and adviser to the Indians. His granddaughter, Polly Copinger, married William Powell, an Englishman, and became the mother of a boy they called Billy. In time, Billy Powell would change his name, for Creek custom dictated that a boy take on a new identity when he reached adulthood. The name he acquired was Asi Yaholo, or, as the whites pronounced it, Osceola.

Little is known about Osceola's childhood, but it was no doubt similar in many ways to that of other Creek children. One white observer who knew the boy's family writes that he lived in a cabin in a small village, as did many Creeks at that time. He and his family probably ate meals prepared from corn and other homegrown

A Seminole boy carries a child-sized bow and arrows in this drawing by George Catlin, an artist who spent many years documenting the life and culture of Native Americans.

vegetables, venison, wild fowl, perhaps occasionally beef or pork, and wild roots and berries.

In Creek society, men and women had very separate roles. The men spent their days tending cattle, horses, and hogs and hunting deer and other game. The women raised the children, took care of the household, and cultivated small farms. Until they reached adulthood, Creek boys helped their mothers with the farming and domestic tasks, and Billy Powell probably helped his mother raise corn, beans, sweet potatoes, and squash on a plot near their home. As he grew older, his mother's brothers may have begun to show him how to use a bow and arrow to shoot squirrels and other small animals. Creeks based their heritage on the mother's family, rather than on the father's, and so Osceola's uncles served as his male role models.

As a young boy, Osceola lived in a cabin similar to the one pictured here. This Creek family has planted corn (right).

Creek boys also engaged in competitive sports. Many of Osceola's acquaintances would later speak of his superior skill at such activities as wrestling, running, and the fast-paced ball game that Indians played throughout the southeast. Creek boys who excelled at these games earned great prestige among the tribe, for the strength and courage they demonstrated in play showed they could be successful leaders in adulthood. This was especially important for a people whose existence depended on their ability to defend themselves in battle. Billy Powell was to discover the significance of warfare before he had reached the age of 10. Indeed, it was war that would bring him to the Florida peninsula and make him a part of that Indian nation who called themselves the Seminoles.

The Seminole Nation itself was formed from a mixture of tribes that had come from elsewhere. When the Spanish explorer Juan Ponce de León first landed in Florida, in 1513, most of the people he came upon were members of the Timucua and the Calusa tribes, who had lived there peacefully for centuries. Over the next 200 years, as European interest in the New World expanded, large numbers of these Indians succumbed to diseases contracted from white colonists. Soon Spain and Britain were vying for the fertile territory, and in the course of their hostilities, many more Indians were killed. By 1710, the population of northern Florida had all but disappeared—except for a fringe of white settlers along the east coast and a few Indian villages scattered in the interior, the region, still claimed by Spain, lay uninhabited.

Little by little, into this void moved a new series of Indian bands from the north. At the beginning of the 18th century, such bands as the Yamassees, the Apalachees, and a large nation of Indian tribes, known

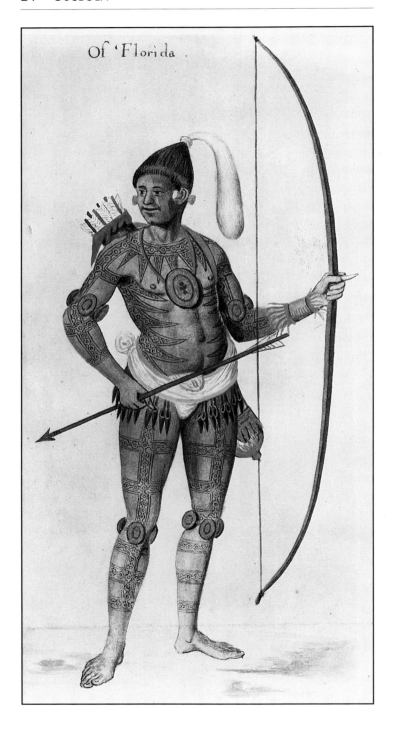

Of 'Florida.

John White, an English colonist, made this drawing of a Timucua warrior around 1585. The Spanish described the early Florida Indians as a tall people with dark complexions. Much as the tribes that succeeded them did, the Timucuas made their living by hunting and gardening.

as the Creek Confederacy, occupied the area now known as Alabama, Georgia, and South Carolina. As more and more Europeans arrived to settle in this region, the Creek Indians and their neighbors began to lose property, lives, and the solidarity that had once bound their various tribes. Driven by the upheaval that came with the white invasion, several groups of southeastern Indians broke away from their roots to start a new life farther south.

The first of these groups, the Yamassees, fled the coastal region of what is now South Carolina after a failed rebellion against the English in 1715. They found refuge in Florida, where the few Spanish settlers accepted them without much protest. In the mid-18th century, several bands of Lower Creeks, displaced by white conflicts around their home in central Georgia, followed the Yamassees south. Some of them fled to western Florida, where they became known as the Mikasuki band. Another group, moving from near what is now Oconee, Georgia, came to settle in the Alachua district of Florida, near present-day Gainesville. Later called the Alachua band, this group was to form the core of the Seminole Nation. Eventually, the name *Seminole*, which historians believe is derived from the Creek word *simanoli*, meaning "wild" or "runaway," was applied to all of the southeastern Indians who came to live in Florida.

Another group of people also contributed significantly to the makeup of the Seminole Nation. African slaves escaping from the southeastern colonies often sought asylum in unsettled northern and central Florida. These fugitives came into frequent contact with the Indians and eventually began to live among them and adopt their ways. Later, wealthier Seminoles would also purchase slaves from their white owners and bring them to Florida to live under a much milder form of bondage than they generally experienced under the whites. These former

Africans would live together in their own villages, cultivate farms, and receive protection from white persecution in exchange for a portion of their crop. They generally took up the customs of the Indians around them, and the Seminoles regarded them as part of the tribe.

Because the Seminole Nation grew out of many separate tribes, its members spoke different languages. Most Seminoles, however, spoke a dialect of either Muskogee or Mikasuki, two languages that are related but not mutually understandable. Other cultural differences existed among the bands that went to form the nation, but in general the Seminoles retained the rituals, beliefs, and day-to-day habits of their main forebears, the Creeks.

The Seminoles shared, for example, a form of government that was also common throughout the Creek Confederacy. The men of each village elected a chief, or *mico*, but the mico never acted without consulting the other members of the village council. This head man was usually chosen from a particular ruling family, but his power came from the respect awarded him by his people; if the people decided the family was no longer producing good leaders, the mico could be chosen from another family—usually one of sons renowned for their prowess in battle.

The last of the groups to enter Florida Territory had been members of a rebellious branch of the Creek Confederacy known as the Red Sticks. Fired by the oratory of the great Shawnee warrior and strategist Tecumseh, these Creeks had adopted a doctrine of antiwhite militancy and the revival of ancestral traditions. Tecumseh believed that the Indians would eventually be destroyed if they did not forsake all the "temptations" the whites offered—tobacco, whiskey, blankets, trinkets, and guns—and fight to regain their old way of life. He did his best to persuade the chiefs of all Indian nations to overcome petty tribal quarrels and unite to drive the white settlers into the sea. Tecumseh gave his followers red-painted sticks to symbolize their unity and their willingness to fight.

About two-thirds of the Creeks living along the Coosa, Tallapoosa, and Alabama rivers, who together were known as the Upper Creeks, became Red Sticks. Between 1813 and 1814 these warriors destroyed cattle, hogs, and crops in a series of skirmishes aimed at starving the white settlers out of Alabama. Their first battle, at Fort Mims, an American army post near Mobile, Alabama, was victorious; of the 553 persons defending the fort, as few as 20 escaped. The triumphant Red Sticks tortured their prisoners, mutilated the dead, and came away from the battle with more than 250 scalps.

The government, already engaged in a war with the British, mustered militia from Tennessee, Louisiana, and Georgia to defend the white settlers. Andrew Jackson, a former Tennessee superior court judge and militia officer, was put in command of an army of poorly trained, undisciplined soldiers and anti–Red Stick Creeks and Cherokees. Known as Old Hickory for his toughness and irascibility, Jackson advanced deep into Red Stick country and won a decisive battle at the Indian village of Tohopeka, or Horseshoe Bend, in the northeast corner of present Tallapoosa County, Alabama. Out of the 800 Indians defending the town, 557 were killed. The Red Sticks were forced to surrender, and in 1814 Jackson made them sign a treaty so harsh that one of his contemporaries later referred to it as "one of the many gross and shameless wrongs on the Indians which disgrace the American people."

The Red Stick Creeks were made to give up all their ancestral lands between the Chattahoochee and the Coosa rivers—two-thirds of their territory. Homeless and humiliated, about a thousand Red Sticks wandered south, and in the course of their migration, the Native American population of Florida doubled. At that time, many Upper Creek families came to live among the Alachua and Mikasuki Seminoles. Osceola's family was among them.

In 1811, Osceola's great-uncle Peter McQueen, together with an elder chief of the Tallassees, began to take an active part in the Red Stick movement. McQueen, a self-professed prophet, urged his family and other Creeks to join him in defending their Indian heritage. In 1813, word came to the Tallassees that a Georgia militia force was preparing to attack their village, which lay near a Red Stick stronghold. McQueen gathered his family, including Billy Powell and his parents, and escaped with them toward the south.

No record exists of the family's experience during the flight, but doubtless it was a time of great privation, which left a deep impression on the young Osceola. The migrating Creeks, carrying few provisions, faced not only the threat of persecution but an uncertain future in a foreign land. Over a year went by before they arrived in Florida.

The chickee, *with its raised floor and open walls, was the typical summer dwelling of the northern Seminoles. This sketch shows a Seminole home and several household implements, including a mortar and double-ended pestle for grinding corn (center) and a European ax (right).*

Somewhere near the border of the new territory, Billy's father left the family and went east to settle in Georgia. The boy and his mother continued with Peter McQueen on into western Florida, where for several years they led a restless life, vexed by the ongoing conflict between the British and the Americans in that region. Eventually they moved to the Wakulla River, south of modern Tallahassee, and became friendly with the Mikasuki Seminoles at nearby Fowltown.

It was in these surroundings that Billy Powell began to form his identity as a member of the Seminole tribe. Because the Seminole culture resembled his own in most respects, it probably did not take him long to feel at home among his new neighbors. The Seminoles lived in palmetto houses constructed around a common square that they swept clean every morning. Osceola's relatives most likely built similar structures, setting up their accustomed vegetable gardens nearby, and continued to hunt, fish, and carry on with their usual rituals. The soil was fertile in the new region, and game was plentiful.

By 1815, both the Creek War and the War of 1812, fought by the Americans against the British, had drawn to a close, and the Tallassee Seminoles enjoyed a period of relative peace. The calm was not to last, however, for throughout these conflicts another brand of hostility had been brewing, in which Peter McQueen was to play a role. Before Billy Powell had seen his 15th year, war was again at hand.

3

"They Will Not Go"

When Osceola's family came to live among the Mikasuki Seminoles, Florida lay in the hands of the Spanish, under whose patronage the Indians had long lived in relative peace. Throughout most of the 18th century, the Spanish and British settlers in the territory accepted the Indian presence, and the Seminoles traded with their white neighbors for clothing, tools, cattle, and slaves. The Seminoles began to own sizable herds of livestock, and in the luxuriant Florida climate their fruit and vegetable gardens produced food in abundance. Slowly, however, a combination of circumstances caused the protection they had enjoyed in their adopted home to give way.

In the late 1780s, a Maryland man, William Augustus Bowles, turned up in northern Florida and contrived to win a following among the Seminoles. Declaring himself director general of the new nation of Muskogee, he persuaded several bands of Mikasuki Seminoles to join him in cattle raids against nearby American settlers. Bowles's empire did not last, but by the time he had left the region, around 1800, his activities had set in motion a pattern of hostile relations between the Florida Indians and the settlers who lived along the Georgia and Alabama borders. Seminole raids continued, and whites who had

Andrew Jackson, having forced the Red Sticks into exile, set out to subdue the Seminoles in 1818. By the end of the First Seminole War, the ambitious general had wrested Florida from Spain.

31

lost livestock to Indian marauders retaliated with raids of their own; relations along the Florida border quickly deteriorated into a long series of small-scale offensives.

But perhaps more alarming to the Americans than the threat of Indian raids was the relationship the Seminoles had developed with escaped African slaves. The Seminole Nation valued its black citizens. Familiar with the tropical climate they found in Florida, the newly arrived blacks helped the Indians cultivate their soil. The black Seminoles also knew English, and often assisted Seminole leaders as interpreters, both in their trade with settlers and, later, in negotiations with the U.S. government. More important still, the blacks were gradually earning a reputation among the Seminoles for their strength, courage, and intelligence in warfare, and they were often enlisted to help defend the Indians against their enemies. Runaway slaves, who had suffered enormous hardship under their former owners, were said to enter willingly into battle against the whites. The Indians, in return for such services, treated the blacks with respect. According to many historians, the Indians allowed their own slaves as well as those who had escaped white bondage to marry into the tribe. Those blacks who did so gained complete liberty.

As word spread that a life of virtual freedom awaited them among the Seminoles, more and more slaves in the southern states fled their masters to find refuge in the Spanish territory. American slaveowners began to accuse the Seminoles of persuading slaves to escape and join them. The whites responded in kind, kidnapping not only recent escapees but blacks who had long established themselves among the Seminoles. Even aside from the anger they felt over the loss of their "property," Americans in the South resented the Seminoles for offering a haven to runaways. As long as this avenue of escape existed, the whole institution of slavery was threatened.

Georgians, fed up with the border raids and the Spaniards' lax attitude toward the Indians and the slave issue, set out to take Florida by storm in 1811. The Americans began a series of systematic attacks on Seminole and Spanish farms alike, plunging the border area into a state of near constant battle. During two large campaigns in 1812 and 1813, a body of Georgia militia and then a company of Tennessee volunteers pressed deep into north-central Florida, destroying farms and villages in the heart of Seminole territory.

Meanwhile, the United States entered combat with the British in what came to be known as the War of 1812. The Seminoles, not surprisingly, sided with Britain, an ally of Spain and the enemy of the United States. During the conflict, the British built a fort at Prospect Bluff, near the mouth of the Apalachicola River—southwest of the Mikasuki area where Osceola's family had settled—and provided it with cannon and ammunition. Although the Seminoles played only a small role in the contest, when the war ended in 1815, the British left them the fort. It soon came into the hands of a band of renegade slaves, and so acquired the name of Fort Negro.

Settlers in the southern states were outraged to learn that their former slaves had won this level of protection. Further, the fort stood in the way of the smooth expansion of the U.S. military. In 1816, General Edmund Pendleton Gaines, commander of Fort Scott, near the Florida–Georgia border, received an order from Andrew Jackson to take command of the Apalachicola River so that supply boats could reach Fort Scott more easily. Although the Apalachicola lay in Spanish territory, Gaines marched his troops due south to Fort Negro and blew the fort to bits, killing 270 of its 300 defenders and further infuriating both the Seminoles and the Spaniards, who had regarded the renegades as their allies.

Alarmed by the Americans' devastation of Fort Negro and other acts of aggression, Neamathla, an elder chief of the Mikasukis at Fowltown, issued Gaines a warning: If American troops again tried to enter Seminole territory, Indian warriors would destroy them. Gaines promptly sent 250 men into Florida to arrest the chief. In the ensuing battle, the Americans killed five Indians and burned Fowltown to the ground, thus beginning the sequence of bloody clashes known to history as the First Seminole War.

It was during this conflict that 14-year-old Billy Powell got his first taste of U.S. military power. Still violently opposed to the American presence, Osceola's great-uncle Peter McQueen had been taking an active part in the earlier attacks along the Florida border. Shortly after the destruction of Fowltown, McQueen led an assault against a boat party transporting supplies up the Apalachicola toward Fort Scott. The assailants killed all the soldiers

U.S. soldiers bombard Fort Negro. One of their shots ignited a store of explosives, obliterating the fort and 270 of its inhabitants.

Neamathla, highly respected throughout the Seminole Nation, was leader of the Mikasuki Seminoles at Fowltown. His village was destroyed by the U.S. Army in November 1817.

defending the boat and captured a white woman, the wife of a U.S. sergeant, in what one historian described as a "horrible massacre."

The U.S. Army would not let the event go unrevenged. In March 1818, General Jackson, victor of the Creek War, took command of the campaign against the Seminoles and, with a force of 3,500 Tennessee volunteers and 2,000 Lower Creek warriors, invaded Spanish territory. On April 12, a segment of Jackson's army surprised McQueen's band encamped in a swamp on the Ecofina River.

JACKSON AT PENSACOLA.

Jackson directs his troops at Pensacola, Florida. Hearing that some Indians had taken refuge in the town, Jackson conquered it, deposed its Spanish government, and set up a garrison, in effect seizing the territory of Florida.

Although McQueen himself escaped, the attacking unit killed 37 members of his band and captured 103 others.

The leader of the offensive later mentioned the presence of Billy Powell—still "but a lad"—among the captives. According to a popular account, while the boy was in the hands of the enemy, an old Indian woman, thought to have been Osceola's grandmother, Ann Copinger, approached Jackson and promised to deliver McQueen if the general released the captured women and children. Jackson complied, setting Osceola and the other prisoners free. McQueen, as it turned out, escaped to the south, to be reunited with his family after spending several months in hiding.

Jackson went on to destroy Seminole farms and villages throughout northwest Florida. That taken care of, he turned his attention to what he privately regarded as the expedition's main business: to take Florida away from Spain. By May 28, 1818, he had conquered the cities of St. Marks, Pensacola, and St. Augustine—the last Spanish stronghold. The Spanish retreated to Cuba, and in 1821, Florida became a territory of the United States.

Now under U.S. jurisdiction, the Florida Indians feared the government's wrath. Already, Jackson's invasion had ended Seminole security. The northern Seminoles had once been proud, numerous, and wealthy; now they were poor and vulnerable. One Alachua chief told a white interviewer at the time: "When I walk about these woods, now so desolate, and remember the numerous herds that once ranged through them, and the former prosperity of our nation, the tears come into my eyes."

In the areas where the Alachua, Mikasuki, and former Red Stick Seminoles had lived, a general panic set in. Many Seminoles abandoned their farms in the fear that as soon as they put in their crops, the whites would claim their land. Most of the Indians retreated southward to the marshlands, where, half-starved, they survived on venison and flour made from the countie-root, which grew in the damp central Florida soil. Some committed robberies against the settlers, and others, desperate for food, resorted to murder. More and more Seminoles became vagrants in the white settlements or went to work for the whites as farm laborers so that they might survive.

During this time of hardship, Billy Powell and his mother fled southward to the area around Tampa Bay, where Peter McQueen and the remainder of his band had set up a new village. After a brief stay at this settlement, the family moved farther south to Pease Creek, now known as the Peace River, and there established a more permanent home. Their lot in this region was better than that of most Seminoles, for they were removed from most hostilities, and they had access to the game that flourished along the streams that fed into Pease Creek.

Here, in the wake of war, captivity, and restless retreat, Billy Powell officially passed into manhood. According to Creek and Seminole tradition, a boy's initiation took place at the Green Corn Dance, a ceremony of purification, forgiveness, and thanksgiving held every summer in honor of the corn harvest. During this event, everyone in the tribe would gather to dance and take part in a series of rituals. Elders would hold court, considering the crimes and social transgressions tribe members had committed over the past year and generally granting them pardon. Men, women, and children were scratched with needles imbedded in a block of wood to release impurities. Men would gather to smoke tobacco and drink a series of herbal teas, known as the black drink, which caused them to vomit profusely. The Indians thought of this drink, brewed from the leaves of a shrub called the cassina, as spiritual medicine that cleansed and strengthened mind and body. During the black drink ritual, the attendant who served the liquid would accompany the participants with a long, wordless song. This was apparently Billy Powell's role, for the name he acquired on reaching adulthood, Asi Yaholo, meant "Black Drink Singer."

As an adult, Osceola would see the foundation for such traditions slowly drawn from under him. At first reluctant to define his position toward the new white power in Florida, he would eventually lead his people in a furious battle against it.

Meanwhile, the appointment of Andrew Jackson as governor of the Florida Territory boded ill for Seminole–white relations. White traders played on the Seminoles' fears of U.S. intrusion, spreading rumors that Jackson would wipe out the Indians or force them to sell their lands for a pittance and migrate to the hot swampy tip of southern Florida.

Frightened by these rumors, Micanopy, a prominent chief among the Alachua Seminoles, set out to learn once and for all what the new administration planned for his people. In July 1821, he persuaded two trusted white men to approach Jackson and negotiate a treaty with the U.S. government. Jackson ordered these men imprisoned as "self made" Indian agents and refused to speak with

Micanopy. There would be no treaties with the Indians during his tenure as governor.

The Indians waited in apprehension. Finally, in April 1822, William Pope Du Val—a likable, humorous Kentuckian—succeeded Jackson as governor. Du Val arranged for a meeting between representatives of the government and all the Florida Indians to be held at Moultrie Creek near St. Augustine. As many as 350 Seminoles made the journey, and on September 6, 1823, talks began.

These negotiations, which culminated in the Treaty of Moultrie Creek, determined the Seminoles' fate for years to come. To the Indians' great disadvantage, the U.S. government had not at this point developed an Indian policy. Some members of Congress wanted to grant the Seminoles all the rights of U.S. citizenship and encourage the tribes to assimilate into the dominant white culture. Andrew Jackson and his supporters wanted to see the

Every summer, Indians throughout the Southeast took part in a ritual known as the Green Corn Dance. In this picture, the near-ripe corn boils in a kettle (center) while medicine men, their bodies painted white with clay, dance around it, singing a song of thanksgiving. A circle of wooden bowls has been laid out in preparation for the feast.

Seminoles removed from their Florida villages and given a place on the Creek reservation in Georgia. President James Monroe waffled between both options. Gradually the notion evolved that the Seminoles might be granted their own reservation somewhere within Florida Territory.

According to Joshua Nichols Glenn, a St. Augustine clergyman who witnessed the meeting, the Indians met the U.S. commissioners

> in a body with a White Flag flying—beating a little thing Similar to a Drum and Singing a kind of a Song and at the end of every appearant verse one of them gave a Shrill hoop—which was succeeded by a loud and universal Scream from them all—in this way they marched up to the Commissioners—with two of them in their birthday Suit and painted all over white with White Sticks in their hands and feathers tied on them.

Other observers commented on the beauty of the Seminole men, who stood over six feet tall, in ceremonial tunics spangled with silver coins and ornaments. Most wore their hair in two strips an inch wide, one strip running from temple to temple, the other at right angles to it from the center of the forehead to the base of the skull, ending in a small braid decorated with feathers. Many had dyed their hair and eyebrows black, and some wore a half circle of red paint under each eye or silver rings in their noses. A few of the more renowned warriors had elongated their earlobes with heavy earrings.

Thus began two weeks of exacting negotiations. Seventy chiefs and warriors took part in the deliberations. Osceola may have been present, although records make no mention of him at this time. Neamathla, the Mikasuki who had been his family's ally, played the role of head chief during the meeting and argued with great eloquence and persuasion. One of Du Val's negotiators told him that President Monroe, the "Great Father," would not forget the enmity of the recent war unless the Florida Indians

Micanopy, leader of the Alachua Seminoles, posed for George Catlin in 1837. The chief, whom Catlin described as "lusty and dignified," asked the painter to give special attention to his elaborately clothed legs.

united on a reservation. "The hatchet is buried," the white man said. "The muskets, the white men's arms, are stacked in peace. Do you wish them to remain so?"

After two weeks of threats on the part of the U.S. commissioners and pleas by the Indians that the reservation not be situated in arid southern Florida, the two sides signed a treaty. It stated that the Seminoles would give up their claim to the territory of Florida. They would remove themselves to an area of approximately 4 million acres at least 20 miles from each coast, extending from Charlotte Harbor in the north to just south of Tampa Bay. White men, unless authorized, were to keep off Indian lands. The government would also pay the Seminoles an annuity (a yearly sum of money) and provide them with farming implements, a school, a blacksmith, and a gunsmith. In return—and this was a major concession—the Seminoles agreed to discourage runaway slaves from seeking asylum on their reservation.

Having achieved a settlement, the Seminoles and the

Fort Brooke, a U.S. Army base on Tampa Bay, became an important outpost during the Second Seminole War. The post was built at the urging of Florida governor William Pope Du Val, who wanted the U.S. Army to expand its control over the southern Seminoles.

commissioners parted amicably. But for the United States, securing an agreement and getting the tribes to move to the reservation proved to be two different things. Seminole migration was slow. Micanopy, who had taken an active part in negotiating the treaty, encouraged his people to cooperate with the authorities, and many of the Alachua Seminoles did resettle during the year that followed the meeting at Moultrie Creek. But many Indians saw no reason to leave the land they believed was theirs by rights. By July 1824, to the government's dismay, only 1,500 Indians had actually moved to the land in central Florida.

Governor Du Val traveled the length of the peninsula trying to persuade the various tribes to give up their lands and set up villages within the bounds of the reservation. Finally he determined that "they will not go unless the United States shows a disposition to compel obedience." He suggested that the army build a fort on Tampa Bay for that purpose.

In the spring of 1824, Lieutenant Colonel Harvey Brooke carried out Du Val's plan, leading four companies of men on the long journey along the Gulf coast from Pensacola to Tampa Bay. They established a garrison, which they christened Fort Brooke, and set up a small village where the soldiers went to drink and gamble. For no known reason, these soldiers were never actually ordered to herd the Seminoles north onto the reservation. The southern tribes sullenly refused to move to the new reservation, and in July of 1824 there were rumors of a Seminole uprising.

It was perhaps no wonder that the Seminoles balked at leaving their homes: the reservation, set in the marshy Florida interior, was mostly unarable. Even Du Val admitted that the land was "by far the poorest and most miserable region I ever beheld." Many of those who did find workable land had little time to plant gardens the year of their arrival, and by winter they found themselves destitute. Desperate for food, these Seminoles began to wander off the reservation to steal from neighboring white settlements.

Yet Du Val remained firm in his plan to resettle the Indians. Grasping at straws, he removed Chief Neamathla from his position as leader of the Seminole Nation and appointed another Mikasuki chief, Tuckose Emathla, also known as John Hicks, as leader. The Seminoles did not protest this move. They knew it was Neamathla who had made his mark on the Treaty of Moultrie Creek, and they believed that once he was out of power they were not responsible for any agreement he had made.

Meanwhile, the Seminoles, on the reservation and off, continued to abet runaway slaves; they even demanded that white slave catchers return the slaves they had stolen from Indian villages. White slave owners stormed Du Val's office, accusing him of neglecting to enforce the terms of the treaty. To make things worse, in 1825 an extreme drought ruined many of the existing farms and brought some Seminoles to the brink of starvation.

Despite the turmoil, at about this time Osceola conformed to government expectation and left the Pease Creek area to settle on the reservation. Having by this time attained the rank of *tustenuggee*, or war leader, he brought with him a band of Tallassee followers. Under the general leadership of Micanopy, this band came to serve as assistants to the reservation's government agent, policing the Indians within the reservation and around its borders.

Throughout Florida, Seminoles, white settlers, and government troops continued to clash over land, slaves, and food supplies.

Finally, a delegation of Seminole chiefs agreed to travel to Washington, D.C., to meet with the new president, John Quincy Adams. The U.S. officials who planned the trip hoped the Indians would be intimidated by the obvious strength of the whites. Micanopy, his "prime minister," Abraham—a black Seminole who acted as translator—and six other chiefs made the trip to Washington in the spring of 1826. Little was accomplished during their meetings with Adams, however, and the Seminoles continued to resist the government's demands.

The following year brought another drought, more starvation among the Indians, and continued conflict between the Seminoles and settlers. Something would have to be done soon.

4

The Hatchet Is Raised

Mikasuki chief Tuckose Emathla cradles his rifle in this illustration commissioned by 19th-century historians Thomas McKenney and James Hall. After the government appointed him leader of the Seminole Nation, Tuckose Emathla continued to defend the Seminoles' attachment to the land. "Here our navel strings were first cut," he said, "and the blood from them sunk into the earth and made the country dear to us."

In the 1820s, as today, most of Florida's white inhabitants lived in cities along the coast. The largest of these, St. Augustine, founded by the Spanish in 1521, was at the time considered quite cosmopolitan. Inland, the city of Tallahassee, site of the territorial government, was also beginning to boast a sizable population. In contrast to these communities, settlers had founded smaller towns, usually consisting of little more than a blacksmith foundry, a general store, and a tavern, along the swamps and rivers of central Florida. It was the residents of these outposts who clashed most frequently with the Seminoles before and after the Treaty of Moultrie Creek.

Most of these settlers had migrated to Florida after losing their farms in Georgia, Alabama, and Tennessee. For them, Florida was a place to make a new start, and they did so with an air of defiance. Nicknamed "crackers" for the sound of the long bullwhips they cracked when driving their cattle, these individualists refused any kind of imposed discipline. Andrew Jackson, who had forcibly inducted the "crackers" into his army during the First Seminole War, condemned them as poor soldiers and cowards. Army officers sneered at their small, dirt-floored cabins, which were usually brimming with barefoot

47

children. Few understood the special brand of stubbornness and courage one needed to tolerate Florida's extreme summers, its insects and snakes, and its annual outbreaks of typhoid, malaria, and cholera. One disappointed settler reported that all he had harvested from his farm was forty bushels of frogs and a herd of alligators. An army surgeon, Jacob Rhett Motte, described Florida as "a most hideous region to live in, a perfect paradise for Indians, alligators, serpents, frogs and every other kind of loathsome reptile."

Though they disliked the Seminoles, many of the "crackers," rebels that they were, also resented the military forces sent out to control the Indians. Some of them realized that the government was attacking the Seminoles partly for sheltering runaway slaves. Seeing that troops were being mobilized to protect slavery—an institution they themselves did not respect—they resisted the governor's requests for supplies and men. In the cities and towns along the coast, some of the "Old Floridians"—many of whom were of Spanish descent—disliked the intervention just as much. But this antigovernment sentiment did not stop most Floridians from fearing the Seminoles and coveting their lands.

In January 1827, the territory's legislative council, responding to citizen demand, passed an act making it illegal for Seminoles to leave their reservation. According to the act, any Indian caught outside reservation boundaries would be sentenced to thirty lashes and deprived of his gun. To assuage the fears of slave owners, death became the punishment for any Seminole caught aiding an escaped slave.

In 1828, anti-Indian whites gained an ally in the White House: Andrew Jackson, champion of Indian removal, had won the presidency. Shortly after taking office, Jackson resumed his push for Seminole removal to Creek

Settlers tend a farm in western Florida. The "crackers," as they were called, led a rough life in the new territory, but they remained fiercely protective of their freedom.

territory. The president, who viewed the Seminoles as an annoying obstruction to the progress of the American nation, did not dream that they could ever pose a military threat; he was certain that their protests would be quelled in short order, and that they would soon migrate west, where army forts could monitor and contain their movements.

In May 1832, after passing Jackson's Removal Bill, the government sent Colonel James Gadsden, a young Tallahassee surveyor, to meet in council with a delegation of Seminoles. Micanopy and other Indians who had proved accessible in the past met Gadsden at Payne's Landing in central Florida. What actually occurred there is a matter of much dispute. No minutes were kept of the meetings, and although a treaty was signed, the Seminoles who took part in the council later asserted that the signatures had either been bullied out of them or forged. Some of the council's participants claimed that Abraham, again serving as mediator, had, for a $200 fee, induced the Seminoles to sign by mistranslating the treaty. The document itself, which was not in the Indians' interest, had been written by a badly trained lawyer, and its wording was fraught with ambiguity.

The treaty stated that a delegation of Seminoles would tour a section of the Creek reservation in Arkansas Territory and consider relocating to these lands. If the delegation's members liked what they saw in the west, they would move their people there within three years, a third of the tribes going each year. The government would then pay the Seminoles $80,000 (about two cents an acre) for the 4 million acres already guaranteed them under the Treaty of Moultrie Creek.

Late in the winter of 1833, seven Seminole chiefs, including Micanopy and two other Alachua leaders, Jumper and Charley Emathla, set out by boat for the land promised them in Creek territory. Traveling up the Mississippi and Arkansas rivers, they disembarked at the government outpost of Fort Gibson, in the eastern part of what is now Oklahoma. Jackson's government had already sent three Indian commissioners to meet with the Creek Indians to ensure the Seminoles' welcome. The Seminole chiefs spent five weeks examining the region. Accustomed to the tropical heat and lush vegetation of Florida, they found the Oklahoma landscape cold and uninviting.

Meeting with their government sponsors at Fort Gibson, the Indians voiced their displeasure. "Snow covers the ground and frost chills the hearts of men," Micanopy told the commissioners. "You would send us among bad Indians with whom we could never be at rest. . . . Even our horses were stolen by the Pawnee, and we are obliged to carry our packs on our backs. . . . We are not hungry for other lands. If we are torn from our forests, our heartstrings will snap."

The commissioners were unsympathetic: either the chiefs signed a statement saying they were happy with the territory and would move their people there as soon as possible, or they would not be allowed to return to Florida. After much deliberation and with great reluctance, the chiefs made their marks on the treaty. The commissioners sent a glowing report back to Washington, writing: "The Seminole . . . is by the late treaty happily united with its kindred friends [the Creeks] and forms with them one nation; but is secured the privilege of a separate location. . . . This tribe, it is expected, will remove immediately to the lands assigned them."

Back in Florida, a few bands of Seminoles thought they had suffered hardship enough in Florida and were not opposed to moving. Most, however, felt they had been betrayed. They recoiled at what they viewed as the government's duplicity, and they began to raise their voices in protest. Some of the chiefs who had made the journey west now said they had signed a paper that they believed signified only their approval of the land, not their intention to move there. Chief Jumper asserted that the land had, in fact, been "surrounded by bad and hostile neighbors." And no one believed the delegation had been authorized to speak for the entire Seminole Nation.

Osceola had up until now shown little interest in the events that were so deeply affecting his nation. When Du Val had called for relocation onto the reservation in central Florida, he had, if at a leisurely pace, responded. Settled there among his fellow Tallassees, he had apparently been living a quiet life. He now had two

Abraham, Micanopy's interpreter, was to play a leading role in the Seminoles' successful military ventures. Whites who knew him spoke of his courtly manner.

wives—a common practice among the Seminoles—and at least two children. Far from defying the United States, as one of Micanopy's band of tustenuggees, he had, in essence, been helping the government enact its policy.

But the Treaty of Fort Gibson, and the circumstances under which it had come into being, struck a chord of revolt in Osceola. Virtually overnight, he turned against the U.S. government and began to rally his fellow Seminoles around the cause of resistance.

The Indian commissioners, meanwhile, would hear none of the Seminoles' cries of protest. Taking note of the stir their negotiations had caused, they nevertheless returned with their treaty to Washington, where it was unanimously ratified by the Senate on April 8, 1834.

Osceola, throwing himself into his new role with a fury, did his best to convince Micanopy and the other Seminole leaders that the United States was following a course that would lead to the annihilation of their nation. Abraham and other blacks among the Seminole leadership agreed. The black Seminoles, whose freedom among the Indians was already tenuous, feared that they would be seized and returned to slavery once the Indians began their migration west.

Finally, Micanopy seemed convinced. He and his allies agreed that the nation should fight rather than abandon its homeland for resettlement among hostile Creeks. Although formal relations between whites and Indians progressed as usual, the Seminoles secretly began to prepare for war. Abraham entered into private negotiations with the slaves who worked the plantations along the St. Johns River, encouraging them to escape to the Seminoles. When the last annuity payment was made in October 1834, he saw that most of it went to the purchase of guns and ammunition.

It was at this point that Indian agent Wiley Thompson met with the Seminole leaders at Fort King to impress upon them the necessity of their removal. He hinted that yet another annuity would be paid—a powerful motivation, for after another hard winter, the Seminoles again approached starvation. This time the government forced them to sign a contract reaffirming their acceptance of the Treaty of Payne's Landing before receiving the much-needed money.

Despite Osceola's dramatic resistance to this treaty, Thompson had managed to persuade 16 of the delegated chiefs to sign, and these had promised to bring their people to Tampa Bay for removal the following January. Yet the war leader's challenge had disoriented Thompson. And apparently, Osceola was not finished with the agent: not long after the council at Fort King, Thompson reported that "one of the most bold, daring and intrepid chiefs in the nation . . . more hostile to emigration, and who has thrown more embarrassments in my way than any other, came to my office and insulted me by some insolent remarks."

In response to this transgression, Thompson ordered his guards to drag Osceola out of his office and carry him in irons to the fort. There, the agent reported, he "raged like a wild animal." Thompson knew that confinement, to a Seminole, was the worst form of degradation, but he felt his influence with the Indians would be lessened if he allowed Osceola to challenge him with impunity.

For the first two days of captivity in the Fort King guardhouse, Osceola refused food and drink. He would not speak, but sat staring at the wall. At length, he sent for General Thompson, saying that he regretted his bad temper and that if the agent would grant his freedom he would sign the treaty. Thompson was suspicious; in all probability the warrior would resume his struggle as soon as he left the confines of the fort.

The agent announced that before he set Osceola free,

Coa Hadjo was among the chiefs who had traveled west to survey the land promised to the Seminoles in Indian Territory. Having signed the treaty of Fort Gibson, he had won the guarded trust of Wiley Thompson.

the warrior would have to win the confidence of certain chiefs whose sympathy for the government cause was well known. These chiefs would act as guarantors of Osceola's continued "good conduct." Thompson sent for two of the most prominent of these chiefs, Charley Emathla and Coa Hadjo, and they arrived the next day. These men had signed both the Treaty of Fort Gibson and the Fort King document, and Thompson trusted them. After a long talk with Osceola, the chiefs told the agent they believed in the young leader's change of heart. They said he had even promised to help persuade the other Seminole leaders to sign the treaty.

The general was delighted. Osceola's reputation for, in a contemporary's words, "great tact, energy of character, and bold daring," made him a valuable ally. The agent went at once to the guardhouse. Osceola repeated his promises to help the migration cause, and the agent unchained him, telling him to return within 10 days to add his signature to the treaty.

As he had promised, Osceola signed the Fort King agreement in July of 1835. From that day Thompson noticed an extraordinary change in his demeanor. The warrior began visiting the garrison daily, and the soldiers found his manners easy and affable. One observer noted that "a continuous smile played over his face, particularly when shaking hands with the officers." He even invited the soldiers to visit his village—called Powell's Town by the whites—along the nearby Withlacoochee River.

Slowly, Osceola won even Thompson's confidence. He worked closely with the agent in his meetings with the pro-removal chiefs, sitting in on their councils and taking an active part in deliberations.

As a reward for Osceola's cooperation, Thompson gave him a silver-plated Spanish rifle, a firearm far superior to the obsolete muzzle-loading flintlock guns that were standard army issue. Such gifts to the Indians were not unusual. Thompson had been authorized to make presents to friendly chiefs who might draw more hostile Indians over to their side. Yet historians later viewed this gift as a pledge between the agent and the Seminole warrior—a pledge that ended in bloody betrayal.

In spite of Thompson's perceived success, Seminole–white relations deteriorated steadily over the summer. In mid-June, a party of white men had caught five Seminoles hunting outside the bounds of their reservation. The settlers had overpowered the Indians and beaten them brutally until a second group of Seminoles had come to their aid. The struggle had left one Seminole dead and three whites wounded. Of even greater concern to Thompson was the murder in August of a mail courier, an act that interrupted communication between Fort King and its supply garrison, Fort Brooke. The general, suspecting that the Seminoles had begun to collect arms, anticipated further violence. He redoubled his efforts to persuade the Seminoles to migrate.

On November 26, 1835, Thompson received a chilling report. According to witnesses, Charley Emathla, the agent's most important ally, had begun to fear reprisals for his association with Thompson, and was eager to leave his home for the new territory in Oklahoma. He had just sold a herd of cattle in preparation for his departure when he was ambushed by a band led, rumor had it, by the war leader Osceola. The two had exchanged bitter words, and then Osceola had shot Charley Emathla dead and left his body for the vultures. The money from the sale of the herd he had contemptuously scattered in all directions.

Alarm seized the territory as word of the incident spread. Sensing the power this new leader held, civilians and soldiers alike prepared for an insurrection.

Weeks passed. Then, some 60 miles south of the Seminole agency, Major Frances Dade, a native Virginian stationed at Fort Brooke, set out for Fort King with a company of 108 men. Dade had received no word from the post for more than a month, and he knew that the garrison had only 46 soldiers and a scanty supply of ammunition to defend it. Realizing the fort lacked the men and supplies it would need to quell a Seminole uprising, on December 23, 1835, he resolved to bring Thompson a relief force.

Dade led his force north along a primitive military road that crossed the Seminole reservation. The company's progress was slow. The soldiers found the bridges that had once spanned the Hillsborough and the Withlacoochee rivers burned to charred timbers. Forced

In pursuit of a retreating transport wagon, a band of Indians attacks a fort. Osceola's highly effective military strategy involved cutting off the U.S. army's supply lines.

to ford the rivers, holding their rifles and ammunition above their heads, the men marched for hours in their sopping wet greatcoats. At every point along the 90-mile journey, they felt unseen eyes in the tall grasses and thick underbrush bordering the road.

Indeed, the Seminoles, under the command of Micanopy and his chief adviser Abraham, were carefully following the miserable band of soldiers, hesitating over when to make their attack. Micanopy was waiting for Osceola, his military strategist, to join him. The warrior's apparent cooperation with Thompson and his Indian allies had proved an excellent ploy; the anti-removal Micanopy had been able to keep himself apprised of the army's plans and to buy time to prepare his warriors for battle.

On December 18, Osceola and a band of Seminoles under his command had ambushed an army baggage train and absconded with much-needed food and ammunition. Following this venture, the leader had withdrawn to his camp along the banks of the Withlacoochee. He had one more thing to do before he joined Micanopy.

A week later, at about the time Major Dade and his men were approaching the southern forks of the With-lacoochee River, Osceola and his band of "sixty tall men" slipped stealthily into the underbrush of a hammock—a thickly wooded elevation of land—about 600 yards from the main gate of Fort King. From this position, Osceola commanded a clear view of both the garrison and the Indian agency office. After hiding for two days among the mangrove trees and praying that the operation would be successful, Osceola recognized an extraordinary opportunity.

Thompson and his lieutenant, Constantine Smith, had finished their supper and gone for an evening stroll. They walked through the fort's main gates, passed the agency

U.S. troops prepare to bury the victims of the Dade massacre, in which more than 100 white soldiers met their death.

office, and were headed toward the trader's store when a shot rang out. It came from Osceola's silver-plated rifle. More shots followed from the ambuscade, and within minutes both Thompson and Smith lay dead. Thompson had been shot 14 times. The band then surrounded the store and killed the trader and four of his employees. The warriors scalped the dead before withdrawing to the palmettos and high grasses surrounding the fort. Their surprise attack had been so effective that not one white defender had fired a shot from Fort King.

Meanwhile, Dade and his men were suffering from a cold December drizzle as they struggled to march in wet and shifting sands. But despite the miserable conditions, Dade was optimistic. His troops had passed through the deep forests and forded the insect-infested rivers without attack, and now they were in open "white man's land," only 30 miles south of Fort King. Surely if the Seminoles planned to attack they would have done so when the soldiers were more vulnerable to ambush—as they had been when they forded the Hillsborough River.

Dade turned in his saddle and addressed the troops. "You men be of good heart! Our difficulties and dangers are over now. As soon as we arrive at Fort King, you'll have three days' rest and gaily keep Christmas!"

These words had scarcely left the commander's mouth when a single rifle shot knocked him from his saddle. The column of soldiers came to a sudden halt as a horde of Indian and African warriors, screaming wildly, sprang from the palmettos and began firing into the troops at point-blank range. Fifty soldiers fell within minutes. Some soldiers managed to build an irregular log breastwork (a low defensive wall) from which they could fire into their attackers. A few courageous men stood by the six-pound cannon, loading and firing its heavy balls. But one by one, the soldiers were killed.

By nightfall, all were dead except for three wounded men who lay forgotten among the corpses of their comrades. One soldier, his arm shattered, threw himself into a pond, where he stood with only his nose above water until the Seminole warriors withdrew. Another was killed by the Indians a few days after escaping the scene of the battle. More than a week passed before the other two survivors managed to struggle 60 miles back to Fort Brooke and tell the army of the Seminoles' victory.

5

"A Ruling Spirit"

The Seminoles' actions struck fear into the hearts of citizens throughout Florida. Shocked by the efficiency of the Indians' operations, white settlers living near the Seminole reservation attempted to take matters into their own hands, and they mustered an army of volunteers to safeguard their plantations against attack.

Meanwhile, General Joseph Hernandez, a Spaniard who had become an American citizen when Spain ceded Florida, called up the East Florida militia on his own authority. Having deployed his forces on the outskirts of white plantations in preparation for their defense, however, he found that some of the planters thought the militia would merely invite an Indian attack. At Belowville Plantation, the owner fired a cannon at his defenders.

Territorial troops, described by a contemporary as "undisciplined rabble," occupied another plantation, at Dunlawton, and forcibly inducted its owner into the militia. The soldiers, resistant to authority and new to fighting, proved cowardly in battle. When a band of Seminole warriors attacked the plantation, the troops fled, their retreat only momentarily slowed by the slave guide

General Winfield Scott had proved himself a skillful leader in the War of 1812. In January 1836 he assumed command of the U.S. Army in Florida.

who cried out: "My God, gentlemen, is you going to run
from a passel of damn Indians?"

The Seminoles went on to mount a series of strategic
attacks on the plantations along the St. Johns River.
General Hernandez found himself unable to defend the
area against the guerrilla fighters, who had persuaded
many plantation slaves to turn on their white masters at
the moment the Indians sounded the attack. Soon, a
50-mile stretch between the St. Johns and Suwannee
rivers was devastated, the whites having fled in terror.
The Second Seminole War had begun with a series of
decisive Indian victories, many of which belonged to the
brilliant strategist Osceola.

Osceola first fully displayed his strength as a leader at
the Battle of the Withlacoochee on December 31, 1835,
only three days after the raid at Fort King and the
shooting of Wiley Thompson. At the Battle of the
Withlacoochee the whites and Seminoles "took the
measure" of each other—and the U.S. Army was
surprised to find it had gravely underestimated its enemy.

After the surprise attack against Thompson, General
Clinch had ordered his men to abandon Fort King and
move to his plantation, Auld Lang Syne, which was 20
miles nearer to the army supply post at the town of
Micanopy. His troops lodged in the old thatched slave
quarters, where they were plagued by lice and insects,
while Captain Gustavus Drane built a defensive wall
around the rest of the buildings. The result was christened
Fort Drane. Soon after its inauguration, General Richard
Keith Call, a friend of Andrew Jackson's from the Creek
War, arrived with a company of 550 men. On December
29th, Clinch and Call marched south toward the Withlacoochee River with their troops. They intended to
mount an immediate attack against Osceola and his
warriors, known to be concealed along the river's banks.

*General Joseph Hernandez
had served as Florida's
representative in Congress
between 1822 and 1823.
When the Second Seminole
War began, he mustered
troops to defend the
prosperous sugar plantations
along the St. Johns River.*

Clinch's command included 750 men and a large and cumbersome supply wagon, which slowed the army's progress along the narrow and swampy path to the river. Clinch was impatient—many of his men were volunteers, and their term ended on New Year's Day. The general wanted to go to battle before their "hitch" was up.

Meanwhile, Call, confident that his large force would trounce Osceola's band of warriors, decided to ambush the Seminoles on their own ground. The night of December 30, he ordered his men to camp without firelight—he wanted to keep their position secret. At dawn, however, a confused bugler blew reveille, and dashed all hopes of a surprise attack. Even so, Call decided to go forward. What he did not know was that Osceola had been following his progress for miles and had prepared an ambush at the most likely fording place on

U.S. troops attempt to cross the Withlacoochee River, unaware of the Seminole war band awaiting them on the other side.

the Withlacoochee. Osceola's army of 230 warriors and 30 fugitive slaves quietly awaited the soldiers' arrival.

On the afternoon of December 31, the U.S. Army reached the banks of the Withlacoochee, expecting to find the fording place they had been told about. Instead, they faced swift, deep waters 50 feet wide. Their mistake forestalled Osceola's ambush.

The generals ordered their men to take turns crossing the river in a leaky canoe they had found nearby. Some of the men refused to cross, declaring that their enlistments were up. Thirty began marching back to Fort Drane, deaf to Clinch's rousing speech heralding the glory of the upcoming engagement and the Seminole threat that would, with their help, soon be eliminated. Many of their comrades, however, were persuaded to stay, and slowly, in twos and threes, they reluctantly braved the dangerous currents.

In the meantime, Osceola's scouts had reported where the army was crossing. He regrouped his men and moved stealthily downstream. Some 30 to 60 soldiers had by this time crossed the river and marched about 400 feet into a horseshoe-shaped clearing flanked by a thickly overgrown hammock. The men were resting, their guns carelessly strewn on the sand, while their comrades waited on the other shore for their turn in the canoe.

Silently, the Seminoles moved into position behind the trees and underbrush of the hammock, approaching the army from two sides. When one of the army regulars noticed an Indian, Osceola gave the order—a loud war-whoop—and the Indians and their African comrades began to fire on the unsuspecting soldiers, aiming particularly at the officers.

General Clinch, a prime target on his white horse, came under rapid fire, bullets grazing his arm, piercing his hat, and killing the horse beneath him. He remained

General Duncan Lamont Clinch, who owned plantations in both Georgia and Florida, joined the army as a lieutenant in 1808 and quickly moved up the ranks. One orderly described the 250-pound officer as "fat and lusty, gray and muscular."

undaunted and did his best to calm the panicked soldiers. Men were running in circles, trying to escape the hail of bullets, but Clinch ordered them to form into ranks and they began, finally, to return the Seminoles' fire.

Alexander Fanning, a fiery, one-armed lieutenant colonel, seemed to be everywhere, urging the men to keep their heads. He ordered some to begin building a log bridge at the army's rear, in preparation for a retreat across the Withlacoochee. At one point Fanning stood in the midst of the turmoil arguing with Clinch. According to Fanning, the army's only hope was a direct charge into the hammock. Both flanks were unprotected, and Osceola was obviously trying to force the army to the right, away from the river, to cut off their only means of escape.

Despite the chaos, the officers managed now and again to catch brief glimpses of Osceola, wearing a "uniform coat of our army"—a blue officer's jacket. His reputation for a love of finery was well known, but the generals took this as a display of contempt for the U.S. Army, as it may have been. Certainly, the jacket served the double purpose of allowing him to move into the midst of the soldiers without being immediately noticed. Stationed in the area of scrub pines between the troops and the river, he repeatedly stepped from behind a tree, carefully aimed his rifle, fired, and took cover again. He carried his bullets in his cheeks, spitting them into the rifle barrel and onto a powder charge before aiming and firing. He was an excellent marksman, and his confidence proved a fine motivation for his badly outnumbered warriors. Their strength increased as the afternoon progressed; soon, a third of the regulars had been killed or wounded.

Finally, Clinch took Fanning's advice and organized three charges. As his men advanced into the trees, the fire finally let up, and the Seminoles fell back. It was clear, however, that a decisive U.S. victory was impossible—the American troops would be lucky to survive the attack at all. Call began preparations for a retreat, ordering one company to protect those who were trying to recross the Withlacoochee on a log raft they had constructed. He sent another unit over to protect Clinch's right flank, thwarting Osceola's plan to cut the army off from the river.

Although their means of retreat was temporarily secured, the army remained in a dangerous position. Osceola himself organized the Indians for a counterattack, and it seemed at times that the Seminoles would prevail. Toward evening, however, Osceola received a wound in the arm, and an officer repelled the warriors who had been trying to get between the regulars and the river.

Meanwhile, the bulk of the volunteers still waited on the far bank of the Withlacoochee, refusing to help their endangered comrades-in-arms. Call ordered them to stay where they were—a risky decision, but he had observed that they were building a bridge that might aid the retreating soldiers.

With Osceola's injury, the Seminoles became more cautious. They held their positions until twilight fell, when they and their African allies silently disappeared. General Clinch quickly moved his men over the makeshift bridge and began the long march back to Fort Drane. The volunteers declared their independence and abandoned the wounded, setting off for home on their own. Luckily for the soldiers, the Seminoles did not attack the slow-moving column, and the exhausted men returned to Fort Drane without incident.

The whites called the Battle of the Withlacoochee a draw, but it was most certainly a victory for the Seminoles. They had repelled an invasion of their homeland by fighting, under Osceola's leadership, as an organized army. From this point on, the whites would treat the Seminole threat with respect.

On December 29, Private Ransome Clarke, one of the three soldiers who had survived the Dade Massacre, finally completed the painful trek from the site of the battle to Fort Brooke on Tampa Bay. He had dragged himself 60 miles, wading and swimming across both the Withlacoochee and the Hillsborough rivers. Haltingly and with great effort, he broke the news of the Dade Massacre to his horrified superior officers. This report was quickly followed by tidings of the army's defeat at the Battle of the Withlacoochee.

News of Osceola's deeds spread throughout the country as the national press published stories about the massacre, Thompson's murder, and the Battle of the Withlacoochee. According to reports, Osceola had cut the agent's scalp into tiny pieces so that each of his warriors could share in the glory of the attack. The public blanched in horror.

Army surgeon Jacob Rhett Motte wrote of Osceola as one would an enemy king, saying "he was a ruling spirit among those wretches and exercised with autocratic power the sway he had acquired by his supposed shrewdness and sagacity over their stern minds." Osceola was often mistakenly identified as the chief of the Alachua Seminoles. This was Micanopy's position, one that the tustenuggee Osceola could not have held, but at the time, whites often assumed that any Indian who spoke with authority in the councils or led warriors into battle was a chief.

Osceola, as the nephew of Red Stick leader Peter McQueen, did hold an important position on Micanopy's council. That influence increased as he proved himself a valuable warrior and strategist. He was, moreover, a handsome man, with refined features and a passion for elegant dress. In his youth, he had been admired as both an athlete and a hunter. Whites and Indians agreed that he spoke with skill and persuasion, and he had even learned some English. Observers often commented on his

confidence and intelligence, and many thought him a visionary. It was perhaps natural that whites would mistake him for a Seminole chief: if anyone could unite the Indian nation against their white enemies, he was the man.

Like most Native Americans, however, the Seminoles showed little interest in acting as a cohesive military unit for long periods of time. In the first two months of the Second Seminole War, Osceola had managed to assemble a relatively large, organized fighting unit with himself, Micanopy, and Abraham at its head. It was this accomplishment that accounted for many of the Indians' early victories. Even Osceola, however, believed that the United States would surrender after the combined defeats of the Dade Massacre and the Battle of the Withlacoochee, and that his warriors would be able to disband and return to their plantations and villages. He was wrong. The Seminoles would have to fight as a single army for a long, long time to defeat the United States. Even if they could muster the will to do so, their resources were scanty compared to the boundless supplies available to the U.S. Army.

Public outrage over the Florida losses elicited a quick response from Congress. In January 1836, the government

Seminole violence posed a very real threat to settlers, but after the Dade Massacre and the Battle of the Withlacoochee, it became magnified in the public's imagination. This illustration shows Indians and Africans committing various atrocities against white settlers. In one scene (top, second from left) the U.S. Army charges to the rescue.

directed war hero General Winfield Scott to assume command in the territory and appropriated $650,000 to fund him.

Scott was an able and popular officer who stood six feet four inches tall. Fond of military pomp and circumstance, he always traveled with a military band, a large personal staff, and a luxuriously furnished tent. His men gave him the nickname Old Fuss and Feathers.

The new commander asked that a large army of volunteers be assembled and that ample supplies be moved south by wagon train from Georgia. The United States stood firmly behind him. The South was glad that its interests—the defense of slavery—were finally being attended to; the West was pleased that Indians, any Indians, would be taught a lesson; and the rest of the country rejoiced at the thought that the Dade Massacre would soon be revenged.

Companies of volunteers from the southern states quickly rallied, and the local newspapers sang their praises. A Charleston officer wrote: "Never did Rome or Greece in days of yore . . . pour forth a nobler soldiery than the volunteers from Georgia, Alabama, Louisiana, and South Carolina." Women's sewing circles set to work stitching flags and uniforms, and banks offered loans to the government should war funds fall short of the mark.

General Scott arrived in Florida determined to eliminate the Seminole force in a few months. Congress had already told him to offer them no terms; they would surrender unconditionally or face destruction. Scott was not to negotiate with the Seminoles at all, he was told, until they had given up all the runaway slaves they protected.

It was these runaways—many of whom came from Africa's militant Ibo, Egba, Senegalese, and Ashanti tribes—who were to prove one of the Seminoles' most potent weapons against the white army.

6

"Some Powder and Some Lead"

Osceola's quiet determination is captured in this sketch by George Catlin. Catlin said that in the early years of the Second Seminole War, Osceola "acquired an influence and a name that soon sounded to the remotest parts of the United States."

No sooner had he established himself at Picolata, a town on the St. Johns River, than Scott decided on a line of attack. He would use a three-pronged pincer movement—a tried and true military strategy—and, catching the Seminole warriors between three detachments, surround and destroy them.

Gambling that Osceola was still holed up at his camp on the Withlacoochee, Scott directed troops from Fort Drane to assemble at the northern end of the Seminole reservation, a unit from Fort Brooke to gather at the reservation's western edge, and men from Volusia to mobilize at the eastern border. The first detachment would force Osceola out of hiding, while the other two companies advanced from the east and west, eventually trapping the Seminoles in the center of their homelands.

What Scott did not know was that General Gaines, commander of the U.S. forces in Louisiana Territory, had, on his own authority, moved his troops into western Florida on February 4, 1836. Gaines had not yet received word of General Scott's appointment, and, as western

Florida was within his jurisdiction, he assumed that he was authorized to respond to the Dade Massacre on his own. Probably dreaming of military glory, he led a small army southward along the coast to Fort Brooke, where he discovered that President Jackson had, in fact, assigned him to the Louisiana–Texas border. There was nothing to do but to march back to Louisiana.

Before returning to New Orleans, however, Gaines decided to take his men northeast to Fort King, where he could collect supplies for the journey. It seems likely that he was hoping to meet the Seminoles along the way and defeat them before General Scott's campaign got under way. Following the old military road that ran through the reservation, his army found the bodies of the soldiers killed in the Dade Massacre and stopped to bury them.

Gaines reached Fort King on February 22, only to discover that there were no supplies to be had. He did not have enough rations to support the journey to Louisiana, so he elected to return to Fort Brooke, where supplies had just arrived by ship. With a six-pound cannon and a thousand men in tow, General Gaines again crossed the Seminole reservation, this time following the path Clinch and Call had taken to the Withlacoochee River.

On February 26, Gaines and his men reached the fording place on the Withlacoochee that two months before had been the site of Osceola's prospective assault on the troops of Clinch and Call. Lieutenant James Izard, who was to lead the first company across the river, had just stepped into the water when a shot rang out—Izard collapsed, a bullet in his head. With that, the Seminoles, under the joint command of Osceola, Micanopy, and Abraham, attacked Gaines's company from all sides.

From nine in the morning to four in the afternoon, the Seminoles picked the soldiers off one by one. When

Too impatient to wait for government orders, General Edmund Pendleton Gaines marched his troops to Florida on his own authority in February 1836. He and Scott were bitter enemies.

they withdrew in the evening, the U.S. troops built a breastwork of logs, christened it Fort Izard, and tried to plan a line of defense. But Gaines realized he was facing a defeat on the scale of the Dade Massacre.

At dawn the Seminoles renewed their attack, their bullets thudding into the breastwork from all sides. The whites were surrounded and their rations almost gone. While the men butchered their horses and roasted the meat, a scout managed to slip through Seminole lines and walk the 40 miles to Fort Drane, where he delivered a letter to General Clinch asking, rather obliquely, for help. Days passed, but Clinch and the reinforcements did not arrive—Scott, greatly angered by Gaines's foolish attempt to win the Seminole War on his own, would not allow Clinch to send relief. If the Seminoles continued to attack Gaines's forces, Scott reasoned, he would at least know where the Indians were—an important factor in his plan to defeat them.

After eight days of siege, with 32 men wounded and the entire company near starvation, John Caesar, a runaway slave whose intelligence and fluency in English had won him a certain prominence among the Seminoles, called out to Gaines and requested a parley. It was later said that a party of Seminole chiefs had threatened to kill him for this presumption, but Osceola had intervened, declaring that he favored the move. What better time to negotiate than when the Seminoles held the upper hand?

On the morning of March 6, Gaines and his officers met with Osceola, Abraham, and war leaders Jumper and Alligator outside the breastwork.

Although the Seminoles had achieved important victories, Osceola had reflected on his position and begun to suspect that the U.S. Army could withstand a long war more easily than his own people could. The Indians had sustained great losses and were already feeling the effects of hunger and illness. Osceola spoke earnestly with

General Gaines—Abraham acting as interpreter—and offered to lift the siege of Fort Izard. Further, he promised to cease fighting altogether if the general would guarantee that the Seminoles would not be forced to leave their home. Gaines later reported that Osceola, during this meeting, seemed intent on convincing him that he felt no enmity against the whites. He even paused in his speech to shake the hand of a soldier he had known at Fort King. The general noted that Osceola ended his appeal for peace with a reference to Thompson's killing and the Dade Massacre, declaring: "I am satisfied."

Gaines was in a quandary. He did not possess the authority to arrange a peace treaty with the Seminoles, and yet if he refused their terms, he and his men would certainly be killed.

Suddenly, General Clinch, who had disregarded Scott's orders, marched into the clearing with a company of men. Seeing the warriors standing before the breastwork, Clinch fired on them, and Osceola and the others fled. The first attempt at a negotiated peace had failed.

Clinch managed to save Gaines and his men, ferrying them across the Withlacoochee on barges he had dragged all the way from Fort Drane. A few Seminoles concealed in the palmettos fired on the men as they crossed, but there were few casualties.

Scott did not welcome Gaines's return—in fact, he was furious that Clinch had acted without his permission— but he decided he could use the extra men in his pincer movement. Unfortunately for Scott, when he carried out the plan, the Seminoles managed to elude all three companies. The campaign was an unmitigated failure, and the national press called for Scott to resign.

In February 1836, Richard Call was appointed governor of Florida, and Congress appropriated another $1.5 million for the Seminole War. Call also wanted to lead the

A Seminole war band surrounds and attacks a U.S. military post.

Florida militia, and he requested more volunteers from South Carolina and Tennessee. Scott saw the writing on the wall and resigned his command.

Meanwhile, the Seminoles continued to attack. At the Oklawaha River, near the town of Micanopy, a band of Indians ambushed General Abraham Eustis and his army of 1,000 volunteers. The Seminoles disappeared, however, as soon as the army returned fire. Eustis continued on to Abraham's village of Peliklakaha. He found it abandoned and burned it to the ground.

In April, more Seminole warriors surrounded and besieged a blockhouse near the Withlacoochee. The soldiers defending the post were near starvation when an army unit finally rescued them a month later. That same month, Fort Alabama, where the road from Fort King to Fort Brooke crossed the Hillsborough River, came under almost constant attack. A relief force, suffering ambush along the way, eventually managed to get the men out of the fort. Before he left, the commanding officer strung the front gates to the trigger of a loaded musket buried muzzle-deep in a barrel of gunpowder. On withdrawing from the fort, the column heard a loud explosion. The number of Seminoles killed in the blast was never determined, but the fort was completely destroyed.

The Seminoles, still under the command of Osceola, Micanopy, and Abraham, continued to drive the U.S. troops to the north and east, away from the Seminole homelands. They had planned their maneuvers with great tactical skill. When the white forces were small, they met them head on. When the detachments were larger, the Seminoles became guerrilla fighters, harassing separate companies rather than the entire corps, picking off a few men and withdrawing when their chances of winning seemed dim. The Seminoles supported their frontal attacks by ambushing wagon trains, fouling lines of supply and communication, and thus further isolating both forts and armies in the field. They even made occasional night attacks, something previously unheard of among Seminole war bands. Generally, the Seminoles acted as a well-trained army.

In late May 1836, Osceola turned his attention to Fort Drane and Fort Defiance. At this point, the climate at Fort Drane had been pronounced unhealthy—the soldiers there, as at other posts, had begun to contract malaria— and on July 19, its troops, commanded by Captain William Maitland, began the move to Fort Defiance. They had covered 9 of the 10 miles separating the two posts when Osceola, with about 200 warriors, attacked the long column of men. Maitland ordered a charge, and the Seminoles retreated, but not before five men were killed and six wounded, in an incident known as the Battle of Welika Pond.

Following the attack, the Seminoles occupied Fort Drane and made it their base of operations. Branching out from the garrison, the Indians began to attack settlers, burning their houses and killing their families, while continuing to strike small companies of white soldiers. Governor Call, who had as yet achieved no major victory against the Seminoles, became the target of President Jackson's wrath. "With fifty women I could defeat all the Indians who have been ravaging the area west of the Suwannee," the president wrote. "I wish the Indians would murder every man in Florida, that the women would get new husbands and breed children equal when they grow up to defend their Territory." Call grew more

This 19th-century engraving depicts the swampy terrain the U.S. Army had to contend with in traversing Seminole country. On more than one occasion, the thick cover provided by the Florida marshland saved the Indians from defeat.

and more determined to find the Seminoles' base of operations and destroy them.

On November 17, the governor and a company of Tennessee volunteers stumbled on a large Indian encampment. Taking the warriors by surprise, they killed 20 Seminoles before the band could escape into the forest. One South Carolina volunteer noted in his diary that the bodies of the Indians had remarkably strong and muscular legs as well as tiny hands and feet. He said the soldiers had scalped and mutilated a captured warrior, then hung his body from poles like a dead animal and paraded it into camp.

The next day, 25 Seminoles died in an attempt to counter the whites' attack. Call and his men ordered a charge and pursued the retreating Seminoles to the border of the Wahoo Swamp. Convinced that the Indians were hiding within the heavily forested cover, Call ordered his men to advance. They stopped at a stream, where Major David Moniac, the first Creek to graduate from West Point, stepped forward to measure the water's depth. He was hit by rifle fire and killed.

Call deemed it dangerous to proceed. For one thing, the swamp would be a perfect landscape for an Indian ambush. For another, the army was already low on rations, and ammunition and supply lines would be difficult to maintain in this uncharted territory. Reluctantly, the governor ordered his men to retreat. If he had crossed the stream he might have won a great victory; not far from where they stood had lain an encampment of 600 Seminoles.

Upon his return, Governor Call received a letter from Jackson; he had been relieved of his position. The president appointed General Thomas Jesup—a stalwart, methodical man known by his troops as one who firmly believed that, as he put it, "the ends justify the means"— as commander of the Florida Territory.

This illustration from the American Anti-Slavery Almanac shows U.S. soldiers abducting Osceola's wife on account of her African heritage. Although the story has never been confirmed, it suggests the vital role the slavery issue played in shaping public sentiment toward the Seminole wars.

Meanwhile, in the nation at large the tide had turned, and the Seminole War was no longer a popular cause. Returning soldiers had told stories of the terrible conditions under which they lived and fought in Florida: the diseases, the poisonous snakes, the marches through swamps waist-deep in water. As many as 103 company officers resigned in 1836. One Tennessee volunteer recorded in his diary: "This is a picture of the soldier's life! A life of dirt and toil, privations and vexations, and the poorest pay in the world, $6 per month." Another soldier asked, wearily, "Why not in the name of common sense let the Indians keep [Florida]?"

Osceola's image in the press had also shifted. In St. Augustine, a popular toast at dinner clubs was to the health of Osceola, "the great untaken and still unconquered red man" who was fighting for his homelands. Popular lore had it that Osceola prevented his comrades from killing women and children. A lieutenant named Henry Prince recorded in his diary the comments of a Seminole woman who had been taken prisoner. Osceola, she said, "is a good warrior and a *gentlemanly indian. . . .* He don't take white folk's things—he never has even got a horse—he would be a good chief if he had men—but, alas! the Redsticks are but eight!"

The public had begun to regard Osceola as an honorable warrior. He became a popular subject of paintings, the artist often portraying him in a togalike garment similar to the costume of the ancient Romans. Portraits also romanized his handsome profile. An abolitionist (antislavery) newspaper even went so far as to excuse his murder of Agent Thompson. According to *The American Anti-Slavery Almanac*, Osceola had been married to the daughter of an escaped slave. At Thompson's order, this woman had been kidnapped and sold into slavery. Osceola's murder of Thompson had thus been a matter of revenge, a crime many Americans of the 19th century would have found understandable, if not downright admirable. President Jackson himself had fought and killed a man who had insulted his wife.

In truth, many of the northern states, home to most of the country's abolitionists, were beginning to object to the idea of fighting a people who harbored runaway slaves. Even more citizens wondered why their country was fighting such a costly war in an unpopulated and, by inference, nonvaluable territory. Army officers began to blame the inhabitants of Florida for having provoked the Indians' attacks by stealing their cattle, slaves, and property.

General Jesup, however, remained unswayed by popular opinion. He ordered the U.S. Marines to join in the fight, dispatching them to penetrate the Everglades and patrol the coastal areas. This was the first joint action between army and navy ever. Slowly and methodically, the Seminoles' movements would be contained—no matter what the cost to the U.S. Treasury or to the soldiers who fought against them.

In early December 1836, Jesup led a small force to the head of the Oklawaha River, where he discovered and burned a village populated by runaway slaves and took 41 prisoners. This attack was considered a major victory

General Thomas Sidney Jesup took over the Florida command on December 9, 1836. After his appointment, the U.S. government threw itself behind the war with greater intensity than ever before.

by the white forces, who at times seemed more interested in reclaiming African slaves than in overcoming the Indians. Shrewdly, Jesup at one point attempted to influence southern public opinion by renaming the conflict the Negro War. He hoped to tempt racists from Alabama and other southern states to volunteer, and many responded.

Combing the Withlacoochee Valley for Osceola and his band of warriors, Jesup tracked them, on January 27, 1837, to the Hatcheelustee Creek. There, his troops attacked a large Indian settlement, capturing the Seminoles' ponies, most of their supplies, and 23 runaway slaves, who were promptly shipped back to their masters or sold to defray the army's expenses. More important, the general had gained some revealing information: Osceola had narrowly escaped capture with only three warriors in his command. It seemed, furthermore, that the leader was ill. As it turned out, Osceola's stay at Fort Drane had proved as unhealthy for him as it had been for the white soldiers. He had contracted malaria, a deadly disease.

7

"A Firm and Prudent Course"

By the spring of 1837, General Jesup had learned an important lesson about guerrilla war. In a letter to a friend he wrote: "If I have at any time said aught in disparagement of the operations of other [military leaders] in Florida either verbally or in writing, officially or unofficially, knowing the country as I [now] know it, I consider myself bound, as a man of honor, solemnly to retract it." The general now understood that small bands of Seminole Indians, operating on their own territory, could attack his forces for as long as they wished with relatively few losses. The palmetto scrub offered an infinite number of hiding places, and the Seminoles made the most of their intimate knowledge of the terrain.

Jesup resolved to change his methods. He began to limit the Indians' field of action, moving his troops through the territory like beaters in a pheasant shoot, hoping he could force the Seminoles to move ahead of his army until they came to the Gulf coast and the navy could attack on a second front. He divided the Seminoles'

This sketch by Captain John Rogers Vinton shows Osceola in regal profile. As the Second Seminole War progressed, the Indian leader's image began to appear in publications all over the United States.

homeland into two zones and outlined a plan to push them from one zone into the other, where they could be more easily captured.

Slowly but surely, Jesup's methods began to bear fruit. On January 23, 1837, the Sixth Infantry, operating in Zone One, surprised Chief Osuchee near Lake Apopka, killing him and 8 warriors, and capturing 16 others. Next, the Second Brigade climbed Thlawhathee, or, as the whites called it, White Mountain, the highest point in Florida, where they engaged a band of Seminoles in a fierce battle, capturing 30 Indians and runaway slaves.

Jesup dispatched 500 men to the swamps south of the Withlacoochee's mouth; another company searched the banks of the Oklawaha River for the war bands led by Alligator and Micanopy; a third unit patrolled the St. Johns River. Jesup detached the largest force, under the command of General Hernandez, to the region east of the St. Johns River.

Jesup's victory at Hatcheelustee had led to a parley between Hernandez and Jumper, Micanopy, and Abraham on February 3, and the parties had agreed to a cease-fire. Unfortunately, neither side honored the truce. A detachment of the U.S. Army attacked a band of 600 warriors led by the prominent chief King Philip and his son Coacoochee just four days before the truce was to have ended. The action ended in a draw.

Jesup reviewed his position. He was beginning to see that the Seminoles would fight to the last man rather than leave Florida Territory. So far, no Seminole warrior of real authority had been captured or killed, and only two Indians had surrendered. Concealed in hammocks or palmetto scrub, Seminole forces could hold off armies 500 times their size. The time had come, Jesup decided, for a treaty. But Micanopy, still at the head of the Seminoles, refused to parley.

King Philip led many of the early attacks on eastern Florida's sugar plantations. Contemporaries nevertheless described him as a "good natured, sensible Indian" who wished above all to be left in peace.

Finally, after many delays, the warriors Jumper, Holatoochee, and Yaholoochee, or Cloud, met with the general and convinced him that they were acting with Micanopy's consent. They agreed, in early March 1837, to cease all hostilities and migrate west of the Mississippi. In exchange, the Seminoles and their allies would be, according to the treaty, "secure in their lives and property . . . [and] their negroes, their bona fide property, shall accompany them to the West."

Why had the Seminoles decided to parley with their enemy, and to accept the same terms that they had so forcefully rejected at Fort King in 1834? Although they had suffered no decisive defeats, even Osceola, who had always been fiercely anti-removal, realized that their days

A Seminole woman rests her feet. Seminole women and children rarely entered combat, but they faced sickness and starvation throughout the conflict with the United States.

in the field were numbered. The warriors were eating roots, fallen fruit, and what foodstuffs they could steal from the whites. Ammunition was running low, and they had no money to buy more. Women and children were starving. Osceola, like many other Seminoles, was suffering from illnesses caused by malnutrition and the unhealthy climate of the Indians' camps along the St. Johns

River. Most important, the Seminoles had won a key concession from the whites—their black comrades would be allowed to travel with them to Oklahoma.

Jesup believed that this treaty would truly end the war, granted that "a firm and prudent course be pursued." The Seminoles seemed sincere in their capitulation, and the Africans among them appeared satisfied with the promise that they would not be returned to their white masters.

But the general had not reckoned with the fury of the Florida slave hunters. The Florida press vilified Jesup and renounced the treaty. Observing the uproar, the commander began to recognize the larger significance of his agreement. Allowing so many runaways to migrate west threatened the very institution of slavery, and, as a native Virginian, he could not defend his actions.

On April 8, the general tried to induce the Seminole chiefs to deliver up all their slaves before migrating, and

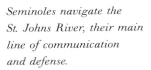

Seminoles navigate the St. Johns River, their main line of communication and defense.

a secret agreement was hammered out in which the Indians said they would renounce any slaves "captured" during the course of the war. Following the meeting, a large contingent of runaways was quickly handed over. But, even as abolitionist members of Congress chastised General Jesup for reneging on the original terms of the surrender, in Florida and throughout the South, citizens continued to clamor that all slaves should be given up. Jesup stood between two camps, pleasing neither. "I will not," he declared, "make negro-catchers of the army." But abolitionists protested that this was exactly what he *was* doing.

Osceola, meanwhile, did his best to promote the treaty, moving his people to a site near the St. Johns River, the embarcation point for the Seminole removal. On May 7, to demonstrate the sincerity of his desire to live in peace with the whites, he agreed to have dinner with one of

This cartoon from the 1840s censures the U.S. Army's methods as they hunt down undefeated Florida Indians. In 1837, General Thomas Jesup declared that he would send out bloodhounds to track Indians who did not surrender. Three years later a successor, Zachary Taylor, made good that promise, causing a great stir across the nation.

the local officers. At one point he also offered to organize a Seminole ball game to gather more Indians into the area. Meanwhile, the army set up another detention camp near Fort Brooke on Tampa Bay.

By the end of May, Micanopy, Jumper, Alligator, and Cloud had handed over their weapons and were living at the Tampa detention center. There, it was reported, they took full advantage of the free food and drink offered them. Osceola and his followers, however, had yet to give themselves up for good, and Jesup was growing impatient. He sent word to the warrior that the army was going to loose bloodhounds into the territory, and that all Indians captured would be hanged. Osceola did not find this message conducive to capitulation. In early June, he shook off his lingering illness and made one last attempt to thwart the United States.

Jesup had heard rumors of an impending attack, and he paid Creek spies to infiltrate Osceola's camp and return with more details. The general also stationed patrols outside the Tampa detention center—but to no avail. On the night of June 2, Osceola and 200 warriors crept to the gates of the camp and, under cover of darkness, attacked the guards, freeing the 700 Seminoles confined there. The abduction was obviously a direct insult to Jesup's authority, and the general did not forgive Osceola for making him look foolish.

The embittered Jesup convinced himself that his entire Florida campaign had been a failure. The only way he could win the Seminoles' territory, he concluded, was to kill every single Indian inhabiting it. He resolved to give up his attempts at parleys and defeat the Seminoles once and for all—no matter what the cost.

In September, Jesup's opportunity arose. A number of runaway slaves, tiring of their life among the sick and starving Seminoles, surrendered to the whites. Slave owners were delighted to have proof that blacks were better off as slaves than as free people. Jesup turned the incident to his advantage by offering freedom to all runaway slaves who abandoned the Indians. At the same time, he told the volunteers and Creek warriors under his command that any runaways they captured would become their personal property.

Aided by a "returned" slave, a company under Hernandez managed to surround and seize a large Seminole band led by King Philip. One of the captured warriors agreed to lead the army to another Seminole encampment, where the general's troops surrounded the Indians as they slept and took them prisoner. With these raids, it was rumored, Osceola had lost most of his men, and his band had been reduced to as few as eight Red Stick warriors. More bad news: Micanopy and his companions Jumper and Cloud had all contracted measles from the white soldiers they had met at the detention center. The Seminole leadership was in decline.

In November 1837, American forces captured King Philip, Coacoochee, and some 70 other Seminoles and imprisoned them at Fort Marion, near St. Augustine. Twenty of the captives, including Coacoochee, were held in an 18-by-33-foot cell lit by a long narrow vent eight inches wide by five feet long. Coacoochee, who was renowned for his swiftness and agility, managed to shimmy through the tiny opening and lower himself to the ground by a rope made of feed bags. One by one, the other prisoners followed. They slipped between the gates of the fort, crossed the St. Johns River, and contacted Sam Jones, also known as Arpeika, the 70-year-old leader of those fugitive Seminoles who had yet to surrender.

Although this daring escape rallied the Seminoles' spirits, it could not counteract the effects of another capture they had suffered a month earlier. On October

27, 1837, Osceola and the prominent chief Coa Hadjo, camping near Fort Peyton on the St. Johns River, had sent word that they wanted to parley with General Hernandez. Hernandez agreed to meet with them, then asked his commanding officer what terms he could offer the warriors.

General Jesup gave an order that would stain his reputation for generations to come. Having decided that the Indians could not be trusted, he ordered Hernandez to ignore the white flag of truce that protected them from capture as negotiations took place. Hernandez, blind to the dishonor such an order would confer upon his name, obeyed.

When Hernandez entered the Seminoles' camp, Osceola and Coa Hadjo came to meet him. Assistant surgeon Nathan Jarvis, who had accompanied the general, recognized Osceola at once as the "principal man." "Nothing of savage fierceness or determination marked his countenance," he reported. "On the contrary his features indicated mildness and benevolence." To Jarvis, Osceola seemed overcome by emotion. The leader allowed Coa Hadjo to speak for him. Hernandez, according to the surgeon's account, gently asked the Indians if they would cooperate:

> I am an old friend of [King] Philip's and I wish you all well, but we have been deceived so often that it is necessary for you to come with me. . . . You will all see the good treatment that you experience —You will be glad that you fell into my hands.

Coa Hadjo kept his guard. Hernandez then called upon Blue Snake, a Creek who had accompanied his party, to say whether he thought the Seminoles should be taken captive. Blue Snake, whose assignment had been to support the white view, instead said that the Seminoles

should be allowed to go free. But this was not to be. Hernandez, whose troops had silently encircled the Seminole camp, suddenly gave the prearranged signal. The soldiers stormed into the camp, seized Osceola, Coa Hadjo, and their 81 followers, and dragged them off to Fort Marion.

Jarvis had been watching Osceola's face at the moment of betrayal. The warrior, he later reported, said nothing and showed no signs of surprise at his treatment. As Osceola had said at the council of Fort King, "There remains nothing worth words."

Captain John Vinton drew this portrait of Osceola around the time of the Seminole leader's capture.

8

"There Remains Nothing Worth Words"

The news of Osceola's capture spread like wildfire. On their way to the fort, Hernandez's troops marched the captives through nearby St. Augustine, and the entire population turned out to see the illustrious leader. Osceola's appearance justified his reputation for personal vanity—he was wearing a blue calico shirt, red leggings, and a bright calico shawl wrapped around his head like a turban. A physician who stood among the crowd recorded that Osceola had accepted his capture with good grace but was obviously unwell.

Soon this most famous Seminole had captured the attention of the entire nation. Although the government supported Jesup's decision to disregard the Seminoles' white flag, the national press reviled him. The editors of *Niles' National Register* proclaimed: "We disclaim all participation in the 'glory' of this achievement of American generalship, which, if practised toward a civilized foe, would be characterized as a violation of all that is noble and generous in war."

A few weeks after his capture, Osceola was allowed to send for his family. John Pickell, a lieutenant stationed at Fort Marion, described their arrival in his journal:

In January 1838, at Fort Moultrie, South Carolina, Robert John Curtis painted this portrait of Osceola, whom journalists would call "the master spirit of a long and desperate war."

97

They came with a white flag . . . and presented altogether a pitiable sight. The bearer of the flag was a fine looking young warrior at the head of the train, which was composed of about 50 souls. . . . The negro part of the train was a wretched picture of squalid misery. . . . They have been on their way a number of days and were much fatigued when they arrived. . . . From the voraciousness of their appetites when they were supplied with food, they seem to have been nearly starved.

The press soon made a virtual hero of Osceola, and when he was transferred from Fort Marion to Fort Moultrie in Charleston, South Carolina, many people traveled long distances to see and talk with him. He received them graciously, sitting for many portraits and talking with crowds of men and women, who treated him with great respect.

General Joseph Hernandez marched Osceola through St. Augustine, then imprisoned him at Fort Marion, pictured here. The army later moved him to Fort Moultrie.

After painting this full-length portrait of Osceola, George Catlin said, "I am fully convinced from all that I have seen, and learned from the lips of Osceola, and from the chiefs who are around him, that he is a most extraordinary man, and one entitled to a better fate."

The U.S. government commissioned artist George Catlin, well known for his pictures of Native Americans, to paint Osceola's portrait. Catlin, who had spent a great deal of time among Indians of various tribes, was deeply impressed by the warrior's physical and intellectual refinement. Calling him "an extraordinary character," the artist painted him in all his finery, with "three ostrich feathers in his head, and a turban made of a vari-coloured cotton shawl—and his dress . . . chiefly of calicos, with a handsome bead sash or belt around his waist, and his rifle in his hand." To Catlin, Osceola seemed to be "grieving with a broken spirit, and ready to die, cursing the white man, no doubt, to the end of his breath." The portrait was considered an astonishing likeness, capturing Osceola's grief-stricken eyes and enigmatic smile with exceptional sensitivity.

Several times, Osceola spoke of dying. The loss of his homelands seemed to weigh heavily on his mind. One visitor noted that news of the war in Florida had a remarkable effect upon the warrior:

> He was told of one [of] the engagements, in which the Indians were represented to have been successful—the effect was electrical—The whole man was changed instantly—He grasped the rifle in his right hand, and while in that position, Mr. Catlin succeeded in taking his picture.—When completed [Osceola] was pleased with it, but insisted that while he held the rifle in one hand the White Flag should be represented in the other—This request could not be complied with.

Osceola seems to have wanted to remind all who viewed his portrait that he had been captured by ignoble means.

On March 6, 1838, General Jesup, having found his strategy, again ignored a flag of truce and captured Micanopy and 80 other Seminoles. Soldiers put the Indians in irons and brought them to Osceola's prison at Fort Moultrie.

Osceola and his wives (left) stand next to Micanopy with his wife, Howedahee, at Fort Moultrie. George Catlin made this drawing a few weeks after Osceola's capture.

Meanwhile, Osceola continued to exercise what authority he retained. Hearing that a comrade had stolen some of the army's chickens, for example, Osceola persuaded the man to hang himself rather than suffer punishment in front of the whites. Visitors noted his fortitude during the last weeks of his illness. Gesturing proudly toward his ornaments, Osceola told one of his guests: "I wore this plume when I whipped General Gaines; these spurs when I drove back General Clinch, and these moccasins when I flogged General Call." Thomas Storrow, another artist who painted Osceola's portrait, dubbed him "the Indian elegant."

Some of Osceola's more critical observers remarked that his pride was always on display—some found his egotism intolerable. Frederick Weedon, the prison surgeon, described Osceola as "a savage in every sense. . . . I could not be made to believe that one Drop of Humane Blood ever passed through his Heart."

At the Battle of Lockahatchee, on January 24, 1838, the Seminoles suffered another great defeat, and some thought the war had effectively ended. The Indians, however, continued to resist the army's removal efforts, and one Seminole declared that they would continue to fight until their homelands were soaked with blood. But while such Seminole leaders as Coacoochee and Arpeika continued to attack white settlers and soldiers, most of the Seminoles who had been captured began the long trek to the Oklahoma reservation.

George Catlin left Fort Moultrie on January 26, 1838, taking his portraits of Osceola, Micanopy, Cloud, and King Philip with him to exhibit with other pictures of Native Americans in New York City's Stuyvesant Museum. On the day he left, Osceola was bedridden with tonsillitis. A few days after his arrival in New York, Catlin received a letter from Weedon informing him that Osceola had died on January 30, 1838. The doctor, who had treated the Indian during his final days, wrote:

About half an hour before [Osceola] died, he seemed to be sensible that he was dying. . . . He made signs to his wives . . . to go and bring his full dress . . . which having been brought in, he rose up in his bed . . . and put on his shirt, his leggings and moccasins—girded on his war-belt—his bullet-pouch and powder-horn, and laid his knife by the side of him on the floor. He then called for his red paint, and his looking-glass, which was held before him while he deliberately painted one half of his face, his neck and his throat—his wrists—the backs of his hands, and the handle of his knife, red with vermilion; a custom practised when the irrevocable oath of war and destruction is taken. His knife he then placed in its sheath, under his belt; and he carefully arranged his turban on his head and his three ostrich plumes that he was in the habit of wearing on it. . . . With most benignant and pleasing smiles, [he] extended his hand to me and to all of the officers and chiefs that were around him; and shook hands with us all in dead silence; and also with his wives and his little children; he made a signal for them to lower him down upon his bed, which was done, and he then slowly drew from his war-belt, his scalping-knife, which he firmly grasped in his right hand, laying it across the other, on his breast, and in a moment smiled away his last breath, without a struggle or a groan.

Osceola was 34 years old at his death. Of his wives and children little is known. They were probably moved to Oklahoma with Abraham, Micanopy, and the rest of the Fort Moultrie captives soon after Osceola died.

Although the majority of Americans supported the Second Seminole War, they also admired Osceola, a man who had fought to the death for the land he loved. Newspaper accounts continued to praise him. On February 2, 1838, *Niles' Register* published this elegy:

We shall not write [Osceola's] epitaph or his funeral orations, yet there is something in his character not unworthy of the respect of the world. From a vagabond child he became the master spirit of a long and desperate war. He made himself—no man owed less to accident. Bold and decisive in action, deadly but consistent in hatred, dark in revenge, cool, subtle and sagacious in council, he established gradually and surely a resistless ascendancy over his adoptive tribe, by the daring of his deads, and the consistency of his hostility to the whites, and the profound craft of his policy.

Osceola's burial, however, was less than heroic. His dying request was that his bones would lie in Florida. But he was buried with military honors within the South Carolina fort, deprived of the possessions that Seminole tradition maintains must accompany the dead into the afterlife. To this day, his grave remains within the walls of Fort Moultrie.

Archeological evidence suggests that Osceola's body did not reach the grave intact. Of the many explanations given for this, one of the most compelling is the one passed down by the family of Frederick Weedon. According to this story, when Osceola had died, Weedon cut off the warrior's head, embalmed it, and smuggled it out of the fort. After the war, the physician displayed the head in the window of the drugstore he owned in St. Augustine. When his children misbehaved, it was said, Weedon would frighten them by tying the relic to their bedposts while they slept.

According to one historian, Weedon may also have stolen the possessions that should have been buried with Osceola: his silver-plated rifle (the gift of Agent Thompson), powder horn, knife, pipe, and earrings. Most of these objects, apparently, Weedon sold to collectors.

In 1843, Osceola's head came into the possession of Valentine Mott, a New York doctor who owned an extensive collection of Indian artifacts. Mott displayed it for many years as the remains of a man "of international importance." Finally, in 1865, the head was destroyed in a fire.

Since 1947, Florida legislators have petitioned the South Carolina government to have Osceola's bones

Weary of battle, large numbers of Seminoles depart for the West.

returned to their state—with no success. In 1966, thieves tried to rob the grave, but the National Park Service, which now controls Fort Moultrie, foiled the attempt.

Before the Second Seminole War ground to a halt, General Jesup resigned amid calls for a congressional investigation of his finances. Following his departure in May 1838, three more commanders—Zachary Taylor, Walker Keith Armistead, and William Jenkins Worth—tried, in quick succession, to subdue the Seminoles. It was not until the Battle of Ahapopka in April 1842 that the Native Americans were pronounced defeated. Congress quickly offered Seminole lands free of charge to any settler who would build a cabin, clear five acres, and live there for five years. The government offered rewards for the capture of the few warriors still hiding in the swamps, and, for a time, sent bloodhounds to track the fugitives.

The Second Seminole War cost the U.S. government a record $40 million and thousands of soldiers' lives. Florida residents, particularly those who had drawn their livelihood from the large plantations along the St. Johns River, suffered enormous losses. The Seminoles themselves were reduced from a large and thriving society to a population of a few thousand people living either in hiding or on a reservation far from their homelands.

For many years the few Seminoles who had managed to remain in Florida suffered great hardship. George Catlin, who visited Pensacola during the years after the Seminole War, wrote of the Indians there: "the sum total that can be learned or seen of them . . . is, that they are to be pitied." Many of these people were reduced to wearing old corn sacks and eating corn that had fallen from the cavalry's feed bags. Some 3,824 Seminoles had been shipped westward by the end of 1843.

The Third Seminole War—a small but fierce resurgence in 1855—left a mere 100 Indians alive in Florida. These survivors hid in the Everglades until the 1880s, when, gradually, they began to trade with the whites again. It was not until 1934 that the Seminoles finally signed a peace treaty with the U.S. government.

In 1911, the U.S. government created two new Seminole reservations in Florida: Dania—now called Hollywood—and Big Cypress. A third, Brighton Reservation, was established in 1935. In 1992, as many as 3,000 Seminoles lived in Florida. Most of them make their living by farming, raising cattle, fishing, and selling crafts to tourists. In 1970, the Indian Claims Commission awarded the Seminoles $12 million for the lands they lost as a result of the Seminole Wars.

Some 20 towns in the United States bear the name of the leader who fought to protect those lands. Two lakes, two mountains, a state park, and a national forest commemorate Osceola. For the Florida Seminoles, as for Americans everywhere, these landmarks serve as an emblem of the brilliant strategist and "gentlemanly" warrior who led his people in the defense of their homelands and helped bring to the attention of the world their valiant struggle to remain free.

CHRONOLOGY

1700s	Creek Indians and other bands from Alabama, Georgia, and South Carolina move into Florida
ca. 1804	Osceola born near Tuskegee, Alabama
1813–14	The Red Stick Creeks fight the U.S. Army; the Creeks, defeated, lose two-thirds of their territory
1816–18	U.S. troops fight Indians along the Florida border in the First Seminole War; Osceola taken captive
1819	The United States acquires the territory of Florida
1823	U.S. and Seminole leaders sign the Treaty of Moultrie Creek, obliging all Seminoles to move to a reservation in central Florida
1824	Andrew Jackson becomes seventh president of the United States
1835	Osceola takes the lives of Charley Emathla and Wiley Thompson; Micanopy and Abraham lead the Seminoles to victory in the Dade Massacre, beginning the Second Seminole War; Osceola obstructs the U.S. Army at the Battle of Withlacoochee
1836	Besieges a company of soldiers led by Edmund Pendleton Gaines; first attempted peace treaty fails; Osceola and 300 Seminoles occupy Fort Drane; Osceola contracts malaria
1837	General Joseph Hernandez, acting on orders from commander Thomas Jesup, captures Osceola, Coa Hadjo, and 81 other Seminoles, violating the white flag of truce
1838	Osceola dies at Fort Moultrie, South Carolina, on January 30
1934	The Seminoles and the U.S. government formally make peace
1970	U.S. Indian Claims Commission awards the Seminoles approximately $12 million

FURTHER READING

Bartram, William. *The Travels of William Bartram*. New Haven: Yale University Press, 1958.

Catlin, George. *North American Indians*. Edited by Peter Matthiessen, New York: Penguin, 1989.

Coe, Charles H. *Red Patriots: The Story of the Seminoles*. 1898. Reprint. Gainesville: University Presses of Florida, 1980.

Garbarino, Merwyn S. *Big Cypress: A Changing Seminole Community*. New York: Holt, Rinehart & Winston, 1972.

McReynolds, E. C. *The Seminoles*. Norman: University of Oklahoma Press, 1957.

Mahon, John K. *History of the Second Seminole War*. Gainesville: University of Florida Press, 1967.

Tyler, O. Z. *Osceola, Seminole Chief: An Unremembered Saga*. Ocoee, FL: Anna Publishing, 1976.

Walton, George. *Fearless and Free: The Seminole Indian War, 1835–1842*. Indianapolis: Bobbs-Merill, 1977.

Weisman, Brent Richards. *Like Beads on a String: A Culture History of the Seminole Indians in Northern Peninsular Florida*. Tuscaloosa: University of Alabama Press, 1989.

Wickman, Patricia R. *Osceola's Legacy*. Tuscaloosa: University of Alabama Press, 1991.

INDEX

PICTURE CREDITS

CELIA BLAND's poetry, reviews, and interviews have been published in a variety of magazines; she is also the author of *Harriet Beecher Stowe*, in the Chelsea House JUNIOR WORLD BIOGRAPHIES series. Bland, who lives in New York, has taught literature, composition, and creative writing at New York University and Parsons School of Design. Of Cherokee descent, she is particularly interested in writing about Native Americans.

W. DAVID BAIRD is the Howard A. White Professor of History at Pepperdine University in Malibu, California. He holds a Ph.D. from the University of Oklahoma and was formerly on the faculty of history at the University of Arkansas, Fayetteville, and Oklahoma State University. He has served as president of both the Western History Association, a professional organization, and Phi Alpha Theta, the international honor society for students of history. Dr. Baird is also the author of *The Quapaw Indians: A History of the Downstream People* and *Peter Pitchlynn: Chief of the Choctaws* and the editor of *A Creek Warrior of the Confederacy: The Autobiography of Chief G. W. Grayson.*